DO YOUR EMOTIONS CLOUD YOUR JUDGMENT? STRUGGLING TO STAY LEVELHEADED UNDER PRESSURE?

Clear Think offers a practical, no-nonsense approach to making better decisions, staying in control of your emotions, and thinking with confidence. Instead of letting stress and overthinking take over, you'll learn how to manage your mindset and stay clearheaded—even in high-pressure situations.

With actionable strategies and relatable examples, this guide will help you:

- Separate facts from feelings to make sound decisions
- Strengthen emotional intelligence and improve self-awareness
- Build confidence by defining your boundaries and values
- Learn to respond thoughtfully instead of reacting impulsively
- Turn past mistakes into valuable opportunities for growth

You don't have to be ruled by emotions or stuck in reactive thinking. *Clear Think* gives you the tools to stay calm, focused, and in control no matter what life throws your way.

WHAT READERS ARE SAYING ABOUT
Clear Think

"This book is like a mental reset button for anyone who feels overwhelmed by emotions or struggles to think clearly." —K.R.

"A valuable resource for anyone looking to improve their mindset and decision-making skills." —S.P.

"Each rule in the book is filled with practical methods that can help change negative thought patterns and improve mental health... the ideas presented in the book are direct and empathetic, as if a friend were explaining them to you" —J.Z

"Helped me with prioritizing my own well-being. As a busy mom, I often feel overwhelmed, but *Clear Think* has been my secret sauce in getting through the day." — Alyona M.

"A powerful guide to mental clarity and focused thinking, this book provides insightful strategies to declutter the mind and enhance decision-making. With a blend of practical exercises and philosophical wisdom, it encourages readers to cultivate a clear and purposeful mindset. A great read for those seeking mindfulness and self-improvement." —Samuel

"This was very insightful and gave me a different perspective on how to make decisions based on facts & data versus emotions." —MD

I like how this book provided useful, non-generic advice that will definitely help my mindset going forward. I would recommend to pretty much anyone looking for a better perspective on life! —Mason P.

"Packed with practical tips to cut through all the mental fog, all the self-sabotage, and helps you make smarter decisions." —Toby

"If your thoughts seem to overwhelm you, Clear Think will give your thoughts something else to think about." —Rebekah

"This book helped me learn to identify my thoughts and when they spiral. It also gave practical tips on helping you control your emotions and thoughts. I found the 5 rules of clear thinking helpful using the I-firmations. I highly recommend this book to others who deal with anxiety on a daily basis like me." —S.H.

"Making complex psychological concepts accessible to readers looking for practical self-improvement tools. The book's focus on confidence and motivation makes it an excellent read for those seeking to develop a stronger, more resilient mindset in both their personal and professional lives." —Rae C.

"This book really taught me how to stay levelheaded in stressful situations. What I liked most is how straightforward and practical the advice is—no fluff, just real strategies I could put to use immediately. The section on separating facts from feelings really hit home for me. I've already noticed a difference in how I handle stressful conversations, and I feel more in control of my reactions. This isn't some deep philosophical read; it's a no-nonsense guide to thinking clearly when it matters most. If you struggle with making decisions under stress or just want a more logical approach to everyday challenges, I highly recommend giving this a read." —Frank D.

THOUGHTBOOKS

Overthink

Middle Think

Big Think

clear think

/noun/

prioritizing facts over emotions to stay objective,
calm, and focused—even in stressful situations.

CLEAR THINK

CLEAR THINK

CLEAR THOUGHTS

LYNDSEY GETTY

THE THOUGHT METHOD CO.

For anyone who just wasn't thinking clearly

Don't believe everything you think.
—Byron Katie

CONTENTS

THE POWER OF CLEAR THINKING

Countless times a day, our bodies and minds follow a natural chain of events. When managed well, this process keeps us aligned with our goals and connected to who we truly are. When misaligned, it can lead to self-abandonment, emotional outbursts, shutting down, burnout, depression, anxiety, and ultimately, a loss of direction. In short, it disrupts our entire lives.

This process starts with our nervous system and senses.[1] Every day we take in millions of pieces of data through our senses: sight, smell, sound, taste, and touch.[2] This information is sent to the brain and communicated to us through our thoughts.

It happens so quickly that we are rarely aware of it. If we were constantly conscious of every detail, the sheer volume of input would overwhelm us, making it impossible to function. To prevent this, our brain filters information, categorizing what is important and what's not.

Thoughts then lead to emotions. So if you hear a loud bang, your immediate, unconscious thought might be, *What is that? Is it dangerous?* This thought triggers feelings of unease or curiosity. The emotions then drive your responses or reactions.

If you hear a loud bang and later discover it was a truck backfiring, you might take a deep breath and move on. However, if a loud bang once signaled an explosion, an earthquake, or another alarming event, you might instinctively check for safety or react defensively.

If you've never encountered a loud noise before, you might look to someone else—like a parent, guardian, or another person nearby—for guidance on how to respond and then mimic their reaction. If you don't have real-life role models or experiences to draw from, you might replicate behaviors you've seen in music, TV shows, movies, or social media.

Since media is often sensational and reactionary, and not all role models are emotionally mature, you might end up mimicking exaggerated and unhealthy reactions because you haven't learned an alternative, healthier way to respond.

This series of events is part of your body's automatic function to keep you safe. When this safety mechanism is working properly, it helps guide you toward your goals, allowing you to feel fulfilled and happy.[3] The problems come when this chain of events is disrupted. If emotions overpower thoughts or if thoughts become skewed, it can trigger emotions that are stronger than the situation warrants.

This is what people mean when they say their emotions got the best of them or that they weren't thinking clearly —though they may not always recognize it.

It can be as simple as someone not feeling like going to the gym and letting their emotions override their goal of maintaining a consistent routine, or it can manifest in more intense situations. For example, dysfunctional parents may interpret a young child's mistake as malicious, someone who's had their trust broken in an intimate relationship may assume their partner is unfaithful without evidence, or a customer may perceive a service worker's enforcement of corporate policy as a personal attack, reacting with frustration or aggression.[4]

Learning that feelings can be mistaken for facts, and that thoughts can be skewed and fuel intense emotions, helps you think clearly. When you think clearly, your emotions no longer drive your decisions. Instead of acting on impulse or reacting out of frustration, you'll pause and make thoughtful choices. And instead of getting caught up in anxiety or stress, you'll stay calm and focused on your goals. You'll feel more in control and make more deliberate decisions, rather than impulsive reactions.

Clear thinking involves challenging unhelpful thoughts and learning how to recognize and manage emotions. This process promotes healthier chain reactions, helping us create better connections between thoughts and feelings. It also provides the self-awareness needed to succeed in all areas of life. And it is what you'll learn here.

The first half of the book focuses on building clarity in your thoughts, teaching you how to identify and change thought patterns that blur the lines between feelings and facts. The second half introduces The Five Rules of Clear Think. These rules offer practical perspectives and tools for managing emotions, as well as skills to continue improving your thought management.

The rules are written as "I-ffirmations"—affirmations starting with the word "I," framing your goals as personal and achievable. By telling yourself, "I..." you create a powerful subconscious nudge to align your actions with your intentions.

As you read the rules, pay attention to the ones that resonate with you most. Consider writing them down or putting a reminder on your phone. The more you internalize these affirmations, the more they'll shape your actions, strengthen your emotional clarity, and help you see results.

Throughout the book, you'll find questions and prompts to deepen your self-awareness and help you take control of your thoughts. Some people prefer writing their answers down, which research shows is more effective for retaining information.[5] However, even reflecting thoughtfully on the questions can be beneficial.

There are templates in the appendix to offer further support. I'd love to hear your feedback: what you liked, what you want more of, and how this book has impacted you. Reviews on platforms like Amazon and Goodreads are always appreciated.

It can be uncomfortable to admit when emotions are clouding your judgment, and working through deeply ingrained thought habits can be challenging. Before we begin, it's important to recognize that this work requires effort, but it's also an act of self-love. Take a moment to appreciate the gift you're giving yourself by committing to this process.

Lastly, please read this in a conversational tone, knowing it's meant to be supportive.

A GOLDEN EXAMPLE

Picture this: Sophia left for two weeks to visit her son and is worried about her daughter Dorothy and their two roommates, Rose and Blanche. While the women usually get along, they sometimes clash when left to their own devices. Let's see how it went:

BLANCHE AND THE GYM ROUTINE

On Tuesday, Blanche had planned to hit the gym, but as the day wore on, the idea felt less appealing. *I ought to go... but do I feel like it?* she thought, glancing at the clock. *I deserve a break. I'm not seeing results fast enough anyway,* she reasoned. *Maybe the gym isn't even working.*

That night she went to dinner with Harold, the optometrist she ran into at the grocery store earlier, but she couldn't shake the guilt. Every dish that came out reminded her she hadn't gone to the gym, and when

Harold ordered dessert, the shame got even worse. *I'm just proving I don't have the discipline. I'll probably fall behind, and then I'll never get where I want to be.* She tried to brush it off, but the thoughts kept picking up steam. *Other people stay consistent. Why can't I?*

The more she thought about it, the more she convinced herself that missing even one day was a sign she lacked the dedication to succeed. Eventually, she decided to call it a week and start fresh on Monday. But the doubt stuck with her. *Maybe I should just give up on all this...*

ROSE AND THE NEWS

That Wednesday, Rose had been enjoying her evening until she saw a story about a series of local break-ins on the news. *Oh no... this is happening so close to home*, she thought, gripping the armrest. *What if our house is next?* She muted the TV, but the silence only made her more anxious. *Maybe I should double-check the locks... or get new ones altogether.*

As the night went on, Rose continued to spiral. Every noise felt like a potential threat. *It could be someone trying to break in at this very moment,* she thought, peeking out the window. Even the sound of a car driving by made her uneasy. *I can't believe I didn't think about this sooner. I've been way too relaxed about safety. Anything could happen.*

Before Rose knew it, she was online ordering motion-activated floodlights. The purchase gave her a brief sense of relief, but the fear quickly returned. She was convinced danger was inevitable.

By bedtime, she'd piled furniture against the front door, just in case. Lying in bed, she replayed the news story over and over, unable to shake the fear. *If I don't stay alert, I'll regret it*, she thought, pulling the blanket tighter. Even though nothing had happened, the fear felt so real that it didn't matter. Rose was convinced she wasn't safe.

DOROTHY AND THE FINANCES

Every night that week, Dorothy sat at the kitchen table, sifting through a pile of bills and receipts. She added up the monthly expenses, and no matter how many times she checked the numbers, the total felt too high. "We're spending too much," she muttered under her breath. *Maybe I should cancel the internet... or stop getting the good coffee*, she thought, tapping her pen nervously.

The more she tried to calm her thoughts, the worse it got, and soon Dorothy's mind wandered to work. Despite receiving glowing feedback in her performance review, she couldn't shake the feeling that something would go wrong. *What if they're planning layoffs? My review doesn't mean anything if the budget's tight*, she worried. *One bad quarter, and I could be out of a job.* The more she thought about it, the more convinced she was that she needed to save every penny. Even the groceries felt like a luxury.

She decided to go for a walk and spotted an Amazon package on the porch—another one of Rose's purchases.

Her stomach tightened. "What did she buy this time?" she grumbled, bringing the box inside and putting it on the counter with a little more force than necessary. *I'm the only one paying attention to this. If I don't stay on top of it, we'll be broke before the year's over.*

AFTER TWO WEEKS AWAY

By Friday, Sophia returned from her vacation to find Blanche doing a Jane Fonda workout with a celery stick in hand, Rose yelling that she needed the TV to watch her self-defense video, and Dorothy eyeing an Amazon box like it contained their eviction notice.

"I leave for two weeks and come home to a low-budget survival movie."

———

The stories of Blanche, Rose, and Dorothy reveal the common struggle of how our thoughts and emotions spiral, pulling us off track and trapping us in unhelpful patterns. Whether it's skipping the gym, catastrophizing, or stressing over money, the root issue is the same—a disconnect between thoughts, emotions, and actions.

And it's not just limited to friendships or roommates—these patterns show up everywhere: at work, with family, in romantic relationships, and even in how we view the world and ourselves.

To break free, we need to understand this cycle and learn to steer it. As we move forward, we'll use the ladies' stories to unpack emotional reasoning and clear the mental fog. But first, how did we start confusing feelings for facts in the first place?

IMPORTANCE OF THOUGHTS AND EMOTIONS

I'm feeling nervous about this. It's going to be horrible.

I didn't get the job. I'll never be successful.

They didn't text back. They must be mad at me.

While I would love to believe Beyoncé when she says "girls" run the world,[1] I know something else does: thoughts and emotions. Even if we try to ignore them, they drive nearly everything we do. Yet, many of us are taught to avoid or suppress our thoughts, and emotions are often seen as a sign of weakness. We're frequently told to "toughen up" or "just move on."

This mindset not only overlooks how essential these internal processes are but also makes life harder than it needs to be. It creates inner conflict, where emotions are mistaken for facts, leading to impulsive decisions that hinder our ability to understand ourselves and make clear, thoughtful choices.

The evidence is everywhere: Who hasn't acted impulsively out of emotional overwhelm, abandoned a goal because they felt they couldn't succeed, or misinterpreted anxiety as a gut feeling?

Formerly referred to as "emotional reasoning," confusing feelings for facts is an unhelpful thought habit that is common in those with depression and anxiety,[2] but even the most mentally well and put together people can fall victim to this unhealthy habit.

Emotions are immediate and powerful, while thoughts require more effort and awareness to process. As a survival mechanism, our brains are wired to respond quickly, prioritizing what feels urgent over what's rational. Without tools to pause and evaluate, we default to reacting based on feelings, assuming they represent reality. Over time, this habit becomes automatic. It makes it harder to separate emotions from facts, reinforcing impulsive behaviors.

The impact this unhealthy thought habit has on your life can depend on how often and where it occurs. While it could be a short-term phase or a long-standing pattern, a single emotional decision can have lasting effects, making it essential for everyone to understand what emotional reasoning is, how it impacts our lives, and ways to address it.

SEVEN KEY CONSEQUENCES

While the primary purpose of our thoughts and emotions is to protect us, they also help us build relationships, solve problems, and navigate life. When emotional reasoning is in play, it disrupts these functions, leading to negative consequences across seven key areas:

Poor Decision-Making. When decisions are driven by emotions like frustration, fear, or guilt, they're often impulsive. Quitting a job when you're frustrated, ending a relationship out of fear, or making purchases to feel better can seem like the right choice at the time, but these decisions often lead to regret.

Relationship Strain. Emotional reasoning can cause us to misinterpret other people's intentions. If a friend cancels plans, we might feel rejected even if they had a valid reason. In romantic relationships, small disagreements can feel like betrayals, creating unnecessary tension and making communication harder. Over time, this can lead to resentment or isolation, resulting in loneliness and missed connections.

Mental Health Impacts. When we interpret situations negatively or assume the worst, it reinforces our emotional discomfort. We might think we're "not good enough" after a minor setback and deepen feelings of self-doubt and sadness. This type of thinking creates a cycle where anxious or depressive thoughts feel more valid, making it harder to break free. Over time, this thinking amplifies stress, rumination, and hopelessness, worsening mental health.

Physical Health and Burnout. Emotional decisions, like overcommitting out of guilt or fear, can lead to physical exhaustion and burnout. Stress from unresolved emotions affects the body, causing tension, headaches, and fatigue. Over time, this can lead to neglecting healthy routines and exacerbate long-term health problems.

Avoidance and Procrastination. Fear-driven thoughts often result in avoidance or procrastination. Delaying a project due to fear of failure only worsens the issue, and avoiding challenging situations reinforces anxiety, creating a cycle of missed opportunities and growing discomfort.

Self-Esteem and Confidence Issues. Negative thoughts tied to emotional reasoning erode confidence. Believing you're a failure after a mistake creates a negative self-perception that's hard to shake, even if there's no evidence to support it. Over time, this undermines personal growth, leads to self-doubt, negative self-perception, and a sense of being lost or disconnected.

Inconsistent or Unhealthy Coping. Emotional reasoning can lead to unhealthy coping mechanisms, like emotional spending, venting without focusing on a resolution, or avoidance behaviors. While these might provide temporary relief, they often worsen the underlying issue, create long-term challenges, and in some cases, can lead to addiction.

These negative consequences prevent us from moving forward and make personal growth harder. They can also lead to self-sabotaging behaviors, where we act in ways that harm our mental health and focus on quick fixes that offer short-term comfort but make things worse in the long run, potentially affecting your life for years to come.

WHY THOUGHTS AREN'T ALWAYS ACCURATE

Our thoughts can easily become distorted, leading us to misinterpret situations or jump to conclusions. Here are just a few common ways our thoughts can get skewed:

- **Bias and Assumptions.** Your brain fills in gaps based on past experiences, not current facts. *You text a friend, they don't respond, and you assume they're upset—when they're just busy.*
- **Cognitive Distortions.** Irrational patterns of thinking can lead to exaggerated conclusions. *After insufficient sleep, it feels like everything is going wrong—even when most things are fine.*
- **Social Conditioning.** Beliefs ingrained by upbringing or society shape your reactions. *You were taught "strong people don't cry," so you feel weak when emotional, even though it's normal.*
- **Projection.** Your insecurities affect how you interpret other people's behavior. *Feeling insecure about your appearance, you assume others are silently judging you—when they aren't.*

- **Limited Perception.** Misjudging situations due
  to incomplete information or hyperawareness.
  *You hear a noise at night and think it's a break-in,
  but it's just the wind.*

Say you're at work, and your boss sends you a short
email: "Come see me." Immediately, your stomach drops.
You think, *I'm in trouble.* Anxiety follows. But what if the
email is about something positive? Maybe your boss just
wants your input on a project.

The anxious feeling didn't come from the communication itself—it came from your thoughts about it. Instead
of focusing on whether you need to ask your boss to
provide more details in emails, you find yourself trying to
self-soothe or wondering why you always feel so anxious
at work.

Since we aren't naturally taught to manage our thoughts,
this lack of awareness easily snowballs.

Instead of questioning the thought, we focus on the
emotion it creates.[3] We obsess over feeling anxious or
upset, trying to "fix" the emotion while ignoring the
thought that triggered it, letting feelings dictate our
actions and perceptions as if they're factual. This is how
emotional reasoning begins. The process starts subtly
and can become habitual over time, especially when
thoughts aren't examined or challenged.

START NOW

Emotions are powerful, but they aren't always reliable, and just because something feels true doesn't mean it is. When we make emotionally charged decisions, it leads to impulsive actions, misunderstandings, and even unnecessary conflict.

To make matters worse, in the moment, we don't realize we're acting based on emotion and unconsciously look for "evidence" to support our feelings, reinforcing emotional reasoning.

When we feel anxious, we assume something must be wrong. This leads to the urge to turn on the news where we'll see 1,000 things to worry about. When we feel unmotivated, we think we're incapable, struggle to stay consistent, and unaccomplished goals "prove" we were right.

The way forward isn't to simply "get over" or push past these emotions. It's about recognizing them and understanding the thought patterns behind them. You walk through the emotions, allowing yourself the opportunity to process them fully.

When you understand your thoughts, you can reshape them and, in turn, gain better control of your emotions. This allows you to make decisions from a place of clarity, reduce emotional reactivity, and improve your relationships. As you gain control, you'll navigate challenges with greater confidence and resilience, leading to more consistent progress toward your goals.

In the next section, we'll talk about how to identify the thoughts driving our strong emotional reactions

IDENTIFYING CLOUDINESS

Before you can change the way you think, you need to recognize when unhealthy thought patterns are happening. The tricky part is that emotional reasoning often feels natural, quietly shaping how you respond to situations, relationships, and even how you see yourself without you realizing it.

Here are some common signs:

1. Making decisions based on how you feel in the moment instead of considering facts or pausing to think things through.
2. Believing that if you feel something, it must be true and acting on it without questioning it.
3. Acting impulsively to escape emotional discomfort, even when it's not the best long-term choice.
4. Letting emotions like guilt, shame, or fear (e.g.,

fear of failure or judgment) stop you from making decisions or taking action.

5. Avoiding important decisions because of fear-based emotions, like fear of failure or judgment.

6. Letting emotions override practical needs or responsibilities, like overspending to feel better or neglecting priorities.

7. Judging your self-worth based on how you feel about your actions in the moment (e.g., feeling "lazy" or "unproductive").

If you make decisions based on how you feel, you might abruptly end relationships due to insecurity or if you feel aggravated during a small argument. Similarly, you might stay out late and have "just one more" to feel better, prioritizing the immediate escape without pausing to consider what happens when you're hungover tomorrow.

Believing your feelings must be true leads to decisions driven by distorted thoughts. You might date people who are bad for you or stay in toxic relationships because you think you'll never find someone else. The fear of being alone makes it difficult to see the clear red flags. And if you have anxiety about your health, you might jump to worst-case scenarios, like assuming a headache is a sign of a serious condition, even though there's no evidence to support it.

Acting impulsively to escape emotional discomfort can have immediate relief but harmful consequences later. You might avoid a difficult conversation at work because you feel anxious or guilty about it and, instead, choose silence. This may feel like a relief at the moment, but it leaves the issue unresolved and the anxiety lingering. Likewise, snapping at someone when you're frustrated might provide quick relief but can damage relationships and leave you with feelings of regret.

Letting emotions keep you from making decisions or taking action will prevent you from moving forward. You might avoid opportunities due to the fear of rejection or feelings of inadequacy (typically misidentified as "imposter syndrome"). This paralyzing fear of failure prevents you from personal growth and accomplishing goals.

Avoiding important decisions also leaves you stuck. You might hesitate to apply for a new job or take on a challenging project because you fear not being good enough or worry about what others might think of you. This fear prevents you from making choices that will push you toward growth and living to your true potential.

Emotions overriding practical needs leads to poor decision-making and long-term consequences. You might overspend to cheer yourself up in the short term, thinking that buying something will make you feel better, only to face regret later when your bills pile up. And who hasn't skipped commitments like a gym session because you don't *feel* like it—even though you know it will impact your progress in the long run.

Emotional confusion can also have negative long-term effects on those around us.

If you're a parent, emotional reasoning can show up as giving in to a child's demands because you feel bad saying "no." The emotional hook here is guilt or empathy —powerful emotions that make it difficult to stand firm, even when you know that giving in might not be the best decision for your child's long-term growth.

This can be true of animal parents as well. We've all seen the pet parent who gives in to their furry friend's cute stares (believe me, I get it), offering extra treats or food, which can lead to an overweight and unhealthy critter. While the emotional satisfaction of making your four-legged (or more) friend happy in the moment feels rewarding, it may not support their overall well-being in the long term.

Of all the negative consequences, basing your self-worth on how you feel about your actions in the moment (e.g., feeling "lazy" or "unproductive") is the most demoralizing. It triggers a damaging cycle that leads to overcommitting to avoid negative judgment, burnout, stress, and a lack of boundaries. You end up constantly chasing external validation, abandoning your true self and values in favor of others' expectations. Over time, this erodes your sense of empowerment, leaving you disconnected from your authentic desires and increasing frustration, self-doubt, and an inability to act with clarity.

Simply put: It steals your joy, takes away your shine, and reduces you to tasks and accomplishments when you're valuable and worthy just as you are.

To break this cycle, it's important to step back and reflect on these patterns. A self-assessment will help you gain clarity on where you're giving up your power and how you can start thinking more clearly.

EMOTIONAL REASONING IN YOUR MINDSET

While there are common unhelpful thought habits, everyone adds their own personal twist to them. Understanding your unique style of emotional reasoning will help you challenge it effectively.

This quiz will help you identify if you are confusing feelings for facts. Be honest with yourself and check all that apply.

Do you:
❏ say "yes" to things out of guilt, even when it impacts your priorities or leads to burnout?
❏ overextend yourself to avoid being judged as lazy, uncommitted, or uncaring?
❏ make impulsive decisions to escape stress or frustration, prioritizing emotional relief over long-term consequences?
❏ ignore how your emotions are influencing your decisions or relationships?
❏ frequently give in to others' demands because you feel bad saying no, even when it affects your well-being?

❏ let emotions like fear, guilt, or anxiety drive your decisions instead of logic or facts?

❏ act on emotional impulses, like making rash purchases or snapping at others, and regret it afterward?

❏ base purchases or decisions on how they make you feel in the moment, rather than on practical needs?

❏ compare yourself to others (on or offline) and feel inadequate because of their successes or curated posts?

❏ feel pressure to live a certain way or buy certain things to match societal or social media expectations?

❏ make choices or purchases to temporarily boost your mood or self-esteem?

❏ act on "worst-case scenario" thinking, even when there's little evidence to support your fears?

❏ avoid making important decisions out of fear of failure, judgment, or uncertainty about the future?

❏ stay in unhealthy relationships because you fear being alone or not finding someone else?

❏ change your appearance, lifestyle, or behavior to match others' expectations or trends?

❏ regret your actions after making decisions driven by emotional urges, feeling guilty or disappointed afterward?

❏ believe that owning certain items or achieving certain appearances will resolve feelings of insecurity or dissatisfaction?

❏ feel emotional discomfort when you don't meet societal or online standards?

Total checked _____ out of 18

REFLECT ON YOUR RESULTS

Many of us rely on emotions to guide decisions from time to time, but if you checked six or more boxes, it's likely your emotions are driving your choices in unproductive ways. Even if you only checked one box, that single behavior could still have a significant negative impact on your life. For example, consistently saying "yes" out of guilt or acting impulsively to escape stress can derail your goals and strain your finances and relationships.

Did you notice a pattern or how your emotions drive you in specific areas, like decision-making, relationships, or buying habits? Are there any recurring emotions (e.g., guilt, fear, or frustration) influencing your choices? How do these patterns impact your well-being, relationships, or long-term goals? If you've identified just one problem area, what negative consequences have you noticed from this behavior, and how does it affect your decisions, relationships, or overall well-being?

_____

_____

_____

_____

_____

ENVIRONMENTAL INFLUENCE

Now that we've talked about how emotional reasoning appears in our thought patterns, the next step is to turn that awareness outward. Recognizing internal habits is essential, but understanding how emotional reasoning is reinforced by the world around us is key to creating lasting change.

Many people are unaware of how external influences shape and validate emotional reasoning, often keeping us reactive rather than reflective. Marketing messages encourage overspending and overindulgence, normalizing behaviors like *"treat yo' self"* and *retail therapy.* Even massive debt is sometimes trivialized with humor, as laughter becomes a coping mechanism for financial stress.

Think about the kind of messages you get every day. From news headlines to conversations with friends, emotions are front and center. Headlines are dramatic, posts are filled with personal stories, and the shows you watch thrive on stirring up strong feelings. This isn't an accident—it's by design. Attention goes where emotions run high, and so the world around you tends to reward emotional responses.

Social media, for example, encourages quick reactions. You see something that makes you mad, sad, or excited, and you're nudged to comment, like, or share almost instantly. There's not much room for pausing to think it through. The faster and louder the response, the more attention it gets. This can lead to the habit of reacting based on how you feel in the moment rather than stepping back to ask if those feelings match reality.

Some podcasters and influencers intentionally provoke emotional reactions to generate views and increase ad revenue (rage baiting). Similarly, some leaders use distractions to shift focus from real issues. As you stay busy reacting to a politician's outrageous remark and getting emotionally invested in party politics, your rights are slowly being eroded.

We also live in a culture where best-selling books encourage readers to manipulate others' emotions and seek attention, equating that attention to "power."[1] As a result, overly reactive and hostile internet commenters often feel rewarded by the negative feedback they receive. If these commenters weren't given attention through emotionally charged responses, they would eventually seek it elsewhere. However, those responding are often emotionally driven and fail to pause and recognize that it's better not to engage.

It's not just online either. In schools, workplaces, and even families, emotional responses are often met with validation or sympathy, which can sometimes reinforce the idea that strong feelings alone are enough to make decisions or form opinions. It's comforting to have our emotions acknowledged, but if no one challenges those feelings, it can solidify emotional reasoning as the default way to process experiences.

Entertainment plays a role too. Reality TV, dramas, and even news shows frame situations in ways that pull for emotional reactions. They're specifically crafted to mimic our internal conflicts so we'll get emotionally connected and continue to binge watch.[2] Conflict and heightened emotions keep us engaged, but they can also normalize the idea that the biggest, loudest emotions are the most important.

You might start believing that if something feels bad, it must be bad, or if something feels good, it must be good. You may also develop the idea that you need to feel heightened anxiety, thinking something bad will happen if you're happy, because movies often portray happy families or lives that are suddenly interrupted by extreme, distressing events.

Even well-meaning advice from people around you can fuel emotional reasoning. Phrases like "trust your gut" or "if it feels right, do it" suggest that your emotions are the best guide. While there's value in listening to your feelings, they don't always paint the full picture. Sometimes, they reflect fears, assumptions, or misunderstandings rather than reality.

It's not just media and social interactions that reinforce emotional reasoning—entire industries, from marketing to politics, thrive on emotional reactivity. Neuromarketing, a multi-billion-dollar industry, uses techniques like brain scans to analyze how people respond to stimuli and replicate the emotions that drive you to make purchases.[3] Ads target insecurities to boost sales, news outlets amplify fear for engagement, and social media platforms profit by keeping you emotionally engaged.

QUESTIONS FOR REFLECTION

How do the environments around you influence your emotional reasoning? How much of the media you consume focuses on drama, conflict, or emotional reactions rather than balanced, thoughtful perspectives? Do you notice how music in TV shows or movies intensifies your emotional connection to what's happening on screen? Is your definition of happiness and love shaped by advertisements?

_____

_____

_____

_____

_____

Your environment reinforces emotional reasoning, and companies rely on your emotions without you realizing it. Whether this is manipulative or not is worth considering, but your primary focus needs to be on building emotional awareness and protecting yourself from emotional marketing so you can stay on track with your goals and values.

By becoming aware of how industries and organizations try to manipulate your emotions, you can recognize when you're making emotional decisions and purchases. Being mindful of these influences allows you to step back and engage in more balanced, reflective thinking. As you go through your day, notice how often emotional reasoning shapes your decisions. Recognizing this is the first step to changing the pattern.

To live a more human-centered life and foster a culture that prioritizes people over profits, it's essential to learn about your emotions, understand how organizations use them to influence your behavior, and gain a deeper understanding of yourself.[4] By doing so, you improve your mental well-being and contribute to a more balanced, connected world.

A NEW VIEW

There's so much in this world beyond your control, yet you're often taught to try and control the uncontrollable. This leads to dead ends, causing stress, burnout, missed connections, and even depression. It also pulls your focus away from what you *can* control—your thoughts and emotions.

When you don't learn how to manage your emotions or mistake them for facts, they begin to control you. Others may exploit this, even calling your emotions a "weakness" to keep you from addressing them.

But when you reject this unhelpful narrative and take ownership of your feelings, you regain your power. By using your internal guidance system as it was meant to be, you find peace in simply being. You learn from mistakes, regulate your emotions without resorting to unhealthy coping mechanisms, and avoid stretching yourself too thin. Being human feels a little less over-whelming. You naturally make space for joy.

Now, let's see how to challenge these unhelpful thoughts so you can shift toward healthier, more effective ways of thinking.

SEEING THROUGH THE FOG

You've identified emotional reasoning, the next step is to challenge it. Challenging doesn't mean fighting or suppressing your reactions; it's about questioning the automatic thoughts that arise and deciding whether they truly reflect reality.

Clear thinking allows you to make decisions based on facts, values, and long-term goals, rather than being led by skewed thoughts or fleeting emotions. By comparing signs of emotional reasoning with signs of clear thinking, you can start to see the difference and move toward making more thoughtful, balanced choices.

Here's how emotional reasoning and clear thinking stack up:

EMOTIONAL REASONING	CLEAR THOUGHTS
Decisions based on how you feel in the moment.	Decisions based on logic, facts, and evidence.
Impulsive actions to relieve emotional discomfort.	Considering consequences and making thoughtful choices.
Assuming feelings are facts and should control actions.	Understanding feelings are valid but don't control actions.
Emotions stopping you from taking action.	Using emotions as motivation to take constructive action.
Avoiding decisions out of fear or discomfort.	Facing discomfort and making decisions based on reason.
Emotions getting in the way of responsibilities, needs, and goals.	Balancing emotions with practical needs and values.
Self-worth tied to temporary emotions (e.g., "I'm lazy").	Separating self-worth from emotions and focusing on long-term goals.

When thinking clearly, you acknowledge emotions but don't allow them to control your decision-making. Instead of impulsively quitting a job because you feel unappreciated, you pause to assess the situation. You might realize that while your emotions are valid, they stem from a temporary frustration rather than an overall toxic work environment. With this clarity, you can plan a constructive approach—like discussing your concerns with your manager or exploring new opportunities—

without jeopardizing your financial security or future goals.

Similarly, recognizing that emotions aren't facts helps you stay grounded. So if you feel anxious about attending a social event, you don't automatically assume that something bad will happen or that you're unwelcome. Instead, you question the thought: *Why do I feel this way? Is there evidence to support this fear?* This shift allows you to acknowledge your anxiety while also recognizing that it might not reflect reality. You might choose to attend the event despite your discomfort, realizing afterward that the experience wasn't as overwhelming as you feared.

Making thoughtful decisions that align with long-term goals requires weighing consequences and acting intentionally. Imagine you're frustrated with a friend who canceled plans last minute. Acting impulsively, you might send an angry text. But clear thinking encourages you to pause and consider: Is this situation typical for them? Could something urgent have come up? This reflective approach allows you to respond calmly, preserving the relationship instead of damaging it over a fleeting emotion.

When emotions threaten to stop you from taking action, shifting your perspective can transform them into motivation. If fear of failure keeps you from pursuing a promotion, you can reframe the fear as excitement about personal growth. Use your emotions to prepare thoroughly, building confidence to take the leap instead of avoiding the opportunity. By facing discomfort with curiosity, you create space for growth and resilience, even when the path feels challenging.

Balancing emotions with practical needs helps prevent them from overriding responsibilities. Imagine you're tempted to skip a workout because you're tired. While rest days are important, you might remind yourself of your long-term health goals. By finding a compromise, like doing a lighter workout or taking a short walk, you honor both your feelings and your priorities. This balance ensures you're not sidetracked by temporary emotions while still acknowledging them.

Separating self-worth from temporary feelings is key to breaking the cycle of overcommitment and burnout. If you feel "lazy" on a day off, you might be tempted to over-compensate by taking on unnecessary tasks. Clear thinking reminds you that rest isn't laziness—it's neces-sary for your well-being. By focusing on your long-term values and goals, you resist the urge to seek validation through endless productivity. Instead, you appreciate the downtime as a way to recharge and show up fully for the things that truly matter.

Thinking clearly helps you create a foundation for making decisions that reflect your true values and long-term goals, rather than being driven by fleeting emotions. Over time, this shift leads to more stability, empower-ment, and a deeper sense of alignment.

There are times in your life when you've already been thinking clearly. Take a moment and consider when you've handled situations logically or made decisions based on evidence rather than emotion. Maybe you calmly resolved a conflict or made a thoughtful decision at work.

Whatever the example, recognizing where you've already applied clear thinking shows that you have the tools to navigate life's challenges with more consistency. The more you identify these moments, the easier it will be to tap into that clarity moving forward.

CHALLENGE EMOTIONAL REASONING: KEY QUESTIONS

Asking questions gives you the space to pause and reflect, allowing you to step back and think more clearly. It shifts your mindset from feeling helpless to feeling empowered, helping you avoid making impulsive actions or jumping to conclusions. You'll start to focus on what you can control and reduce frustration and emotional intensity in the process.

It's not about questioning everything all the time, but about being intentional with your inquiries and making sure you're asking the right questions. This process builds the self-awareness you need to lean into your power and adjust your thinking, keeping it aligned with your goals.

While there are a lot of questions you can ask, there are three general areas you want to consider:

1. The source of the thought
2. Alternative viewpoints
3. Whether the thought is helpful

WHERE DID THE THOUGHT COME FROM?

Thoughts are often shaped by underlying fears, assumptions, or past experiences that influence your present thinking. By taking the time to question the root of a thought and what purpose it serves, you gain deeper self-awareness and challenge patterns that no longer serve you. This also helps separate emotional reactions from rational conclusions, allowing you to make more conscious, intentional decisions.

For instance, to challenge her thoughts, Blanche would focus on why skipping one gym day made her feel so guilty and question the belief that one missed workout defines her discipline. She might ask herself whether her expectations for immediate results are realistic or if they stem from unrealistic standards or comparisons to others rather than her own progress.

If Rose challenged her thoughts, she might examine why she believed her safety depended on the extra measures she was taking. She would question whether her fears stemmed from specific past experiences or a general sense of anxiety—possibly fueled by sensationalized news.[1] By recognizing that her fear might be exaggerating the actual danger, she could focus on practical ways to feel safe without letting fear dictate her decisions.

And Dorothy might slow down and reflect on her childhood experience of nearly being evicted when her father lost his job. She could consider whether her concerns about job insecurity were based on facts or worst-case scenarios fueled by anxiety. Instead of panicking and cutting necessities like coffee or the internet, she might calmly evaluate her budget, identifying small adjustments that make a difference without sacrificing essentials. By recognizing that her stress partly stemmed from fear of the unknown, she could shift her focus to what she could realistically control rather than catastrophizing.

WHAT ARE ALTERNATIVE VIEWPOINTS AND EVIDENCE?

Limiting yourself to one way of thinking can make problems seem larger than they are by preventing you from seeing new solutions and insights. Considering different perspectives broadens your understanding and challenges assumptions. By focusing on evidence, you not only grow personally but also learn to separate current situations from past experiences, enabling clearer judgment and helping you resist external influences.

Blanche can focus on evidence by reminding herself that she has already gone to the gym three times this week. If motivation becomes an issue, she can reassess her goals and set personal boundaries to stay on track. Tracking her progress could help her feel more in control, but it's important to recognize that progress can vary based on how individual bodies respond to exercise.[2] Understanding this will help Blanche stay patient and committed to her goals, even when immediate changes aren't visible.

By focusing on real solutions, Rose can reduce fear and make more balanced decisions. Before buying self-defense items, she could check crime statistics to assess the actual risk in her neighborhood.[3] Learning that crime is generally down might help her feel safer and less anxious. Reminding herself that her home and neighborhood are statistically safe, she could take calm, practical steps—like checking the locks—rather than reacting impulsively.

And Dorothy can focus on the fact that, while layoffs are always a possibility, they're unlikely in her current situation. She can remind herself of the positive feedback her boss gave in her performance review and that she has severance and support from her roommates if things get tough. By looking at the facts, she challenges the fear rooted in past experiences and makes decisions based on her present reality.

IS THE THOUGHT HELPFUL?

Not all thoughts are productive; some can keep you stuck or hold you back from reaching your goals. By evaluating whether a thought is solving a problem, guiding you toward growth, or causing unnecessary stress, you can decide whether it's worth keeping, needs adjustment, or needs to be worked through. This process helps you focus on thoughts that align with you, allowing you to move forward with clarity and intention.

When Blanche thinks about how she doesn't feel like going to the gym, she can recognize that this thought isn't very helpful. Just not feeling like doing something isn't a good reason to skip it, especially when it's important for her health. Instead, she can use the thought as a check-in: Is she physically well enough to go? If the answer is yes, she can remind herself that she's capable of going and needs to stick to her goal. This shift in thinking can help her take action even when she lacks motivation.

Rose can manage her fears by questioning whether her thoughts are helpful or just adding unnecessary stress. When she feels anxious about her safety, she can remind herself that it's natural to worry about staying safe, but it doesn't have to consume her or cause overwhelming anxiety. Instead of piling furniture against the door or buying unnecessary floodlights, she can focus on practical steps, like double-checking the locks. By managing unproductive thoughts and focusing on realistic solutions, Rose will feel safer and more in control without being consumed by fear.

And it's not healthy for Dorothy to constantly worry about negative "what ifs." Instead, she can focus on the present and redirect her attention when unhelpful thoughts come up. If she struggles to quiet her worries, she can imagine more positive "what if" scenarios, like what she would do if she won the lottery. While winning the lottery is unlikely (and she definitely shouldn't spend all her money on lottery tickets), positive "what ifs" can make unhelpful thoughts feel lighter and more manageable, offering a helpful shift in perspective.

Reflect on the emotional pattern you identified earlier in the self-assessment. Where is this emotion coming from: past experiences, assumptions, or a current situation? Is this thought or emotion helping you move forward toward your goals, or is it creating unnecessary stress or impulsive reactions? Consider whether there are alternative viewpoints or evidence that could help you look at the situation differently.

_____

_____

_____

_____

_____

By asking diverse questions, you give yourself multiple entry points to challenge your thoughts in a meaningful way. Over time, this practice will help shift emotional reasoning into a more balanced, thoughtful approach.

UNDERSTANDING EMOTIONAL PROFITING

Asking who profits from our emotions is important because many industries rely on emotional reactions to influence our decisions. Most companies wouldn't be able to exist without us, and they spend billions of dollars to understand what will make us buy, click, and stay on their platforms the longest. They target feelings like fear, insecurity, or excitement to sell products, gain support, or hold our attention.

Common advice for creating a successful social media reel is to include an emotional hook that grabs viewers' attention and triggers a reaction, whether it's curiosity, excitement, or even empathy. The diet industry thrives when people feel discouraged or overwhelmed. When you believe your efforts aren't enough, they're ready to sell you "quick fixes" that promise fast results. And news outlets use emotions like envy or fear to keep you engaged, making it harder to step away or think critically about their influence.

By understanding how industries profit from your emotions, you identify manipulative strategies and regain control over your decisions. This awareness helps you protect your time, energy, and well-being, allowing you to focus on what truly matters instead of being swayed by emotional appeals. Here are how some organizations profit from your emotions:

Advertising & Shopping: Ads drive purchases

through self-worth & insecurity. *"Buy this luxury skincare product because you deserve to feel beautiful."* Instead of asking if the product is necessary, people buy to avoid guilt or feeling neglected.

Social Media: Curated, "perfect" lives online fuel comparison & self-doubt. People change their habits, make purchases, or even alter their appearance to "keep up," despite lacking real evidence their lives are inadequate.

Diet Industry: Quick-fix diets and supplements take advantage of people's doubts and struggles. They promise fast, unrealistic results, keeping people stuck in a loop of failure and spending instead of building long-term health.

News & Media: Sensational headlines trigger fear & urgency. *"Killer Storm Threatens Millions: Your Town Could Be Next!"* People stay glued to alarming stories designed to provoke anxiety.

Addiction Industries: Gambling, alcohol, and junk food profit from emotional avoidance. They sell the promise of fun, relaxation, or comfort, keeping people hooked on quick relief instead of facing their underlying feelings.

Politics: Fear-based messages use control and play on anxiety to shape opinions. "If you don't vote for this, your family won't be safe." Instead of looking critically at policies, people react emotionally and connect their identity to political beliefs.

Pharmaceutical Industry: Drug companies profit from fear and hope. While medication has its place, ads push drugs as the first solution, making people believe they need a pill for every problem instead of exploring other options for long-term health.

How can you recognize and minimize the impact of emotional hooks used by industries like advertising, social media, or news outlets to influence your decisions? Consider specific strategies (like reducing exposure) to protect your emotional well-being.

_____

_____

_____

_____

_____

A WHOLE NEW WORLD

The more you challenge emotional reasoning, the easier it is to recognize when your feelings are clouding your judgment. While companies and organizations won't change their tactics, you'll be more aware of their manipulative strategies. Over time, you'll get better at separating your emotions from the facts and make clearer, more rational choices.

Instead of getting teary-eyed over a commercial that depicts a cozy family gathering, you'll realize that it was specifically curated to trigger an emotional response and create a connection to a product. Similarly, when the news tells you "no one is safe,"[4] you'll be able to step back and stop reacting out of fear. Instead, your outrage will shift to the real issue: the lack of fact-based reporting and the spreading of fear for profit.

By consistently challenging emotional reasoning, you don't just make better decisions—you change the way you see the world and how you engage with organizations that are designed to manipulate your emotions. You stop being a passive consumer and start becoming more conscious of the messages you're receiving. This shift empowers you to respond to situations thoughtfully, instead of being swept up by emotional reactions. In the end, it's about reclaiming control over your choices and aligning them with what truly matters to you, not just what's being sold.

EVALUATING THE BENEFITS

After identifying an emotion that's mistaken for a fact and the thought behind it, you can often reduce its intensity and think more clearly by simply challenging it. For example, if you feel flustered and realize that most things on your to-do list aren't as urgent as you originally thought, you can prioritize your tasks and tackle the most important ones first. Or if you think someone was rude but later realize your negative interpretation might be due to being hungry, you can eat something and give yourself a chance to think more clearly.

But if a thought is deeply rooted or part of a larger pattern, like always assuming the worst in social situations or feeling like you're falling behind in life, reframing it might take more effort. This is where evaluating the benefits comes in. When you focus on how responding with clarity will improve your future, it becomes easier to stay focused on long-term goals. With this future-focused mindset, you'll be better able to move past impulsive reactions or demotivating thoughts that keep you from staying on track.

To evaluate, focus on three key things:

1. Actions you can take to improve your situation
2. How reducing emotional reasoning helps you achieve your goals (and how good that will feel)
3. The obstacles that are preventing change

Let's see how this works for Dorothy, Rose, and Blanche:

HEALTH CONSCIOUS BLANCHE

Blanche can improve her situation by organizing her goals more effectively. Focusing on external validation often leads to failure because it lacks a true desire for change. If her goal is to lose weight simply to keep up with younger women in the dating scene, she'll likely struggle to achieve it. However, if Blanche realizes she wants to feel healthier and stay fit as she ages, she can create a routine that works for her.

If Blanche realizes she's too tired after work to go to the gym, she could try going earlier in the day and commit to at least three days a week, unless she's really sick or exhausted. Finding an accountability partner could also help keep her motivated. By focusing on how good she'll feel after the gym, rather than the difficulty of going now, she can reinforce her routine. Reducing emotional reasoning will help her honor her goals and feel proud of maintaining her boundaries, making it easier to stay motivated in the long run.

Blanche could also assess what's really stopping her from changing. For example, maybe she's eating cheesecake with her roommates during late-night talks. While she doesn't need to skip the midnight chats, she could replace the cheesecake with fruit or a healthy snack. This way, she can still enjoy her time with her roommates without sabotaging her health goals. If she doesn't feel like eating healthier alternatives, then she can identify and challenge the thoughts behind the feeling.

BLACK BELT ROSE

It's unlikely that Rose's goal is to barricade her house and cause tension with her roommates. To evaluate, she can consider what her real goal is with the home security system. If it's to feel safe, she can remind herself that the news often sensationalizes crime and rarely highlights the positives, so the information she sees does not reflect reality.[1] She can also focus on what she can control, helping her avoid getting caught up in things she can't change. Instead of living in fear, she could focus on enjoying life, learning new skills, or reconnecting with friends back home in St. Olaf.

When she stops herself from being driven by news-manufactured fear, she might even realize that she likes doing self-defense workouts and that she wants to continue practicing self-defense or martial arts because she enjoys it.

As for what's stopping her from changing, Rose could remind herself that buying things provides only temporary comfort. Instead of relying on purchases for happiness, she can reassess her priorities and focus on positive activities that truly bring joy, like connecting with loved ones or pursuing hobbies. By focusing on long-term goals, she can move away from the instant gratification of clicking "buy."

ZEN DOROTHY

To improve her situation, Dorothy might need to stop being so rigid about her finances. While it's important to have a budget, not every dime needs to be tracked perfectly, and constantly tracking every expense can lead to unnecessary stress. She can consider using tracking apps to manage her money and save herself time.

Dorothy could also focus on her work performance and consider ways to improve and advance her career if that's her goal. If she wants extra income, she can consider if she has the time and energy for a side hustle.

If her goal is to feel financially secure, not worrying that a simple Amazon delivery will lead to eviction will help her think more clearly about her situation. By focusing on how good it will feel to have more freedom from financial stress, she can let go of unnecessary worries.

Dorothy can also consider if she is avoiding important financial conversations with her roommates, that, if had, could relieve her stress and help her feel more at ease with her financial situation. If she realizes she is uncomfortable talking about finances she can reflect on what specifically makes her uneasy, challenge any fears or assumptions she has about discussing money, and practice having small, low-stakes conversations to build confidence. She can also set a time with her roommates to talk openly about shared expenses to reduce uncertainty and make sure everyone is on the same page.

WHAT DOES YOUR FUTURE LOOK LIKE?

Think back to a time when you abandoned a goal because you didn't feel you could accomplish it or reflect on moments when you confused your feelings for facts. How could focusing on the future, instead of getting caught up in those emotions, help you think more clearly and make better decisions moving forward? How has your perspective changed since you started this process? What areas of your life feel clearer now?

_____

_____

_____

_____

_____

While companies and organizations may not change overnight, it's worth imagining a world where you aren't constantly urged to make emotional purchases. Ads would focus on providing clear, useful information about products. Social media would create real connections instead of promoting curated, idealized images. The news would prioritize balanced, fact-based reporting over fear and outrage.

How might your daily life and decisions change if you were less influenced by emotional triggers in advertising, social media, and news, and instead were provided with more transparent, balanced, and fact-based information?

_____

_____

_____

_____

_____

FUTURE CONTROL

People often talk about the future as if it's distant, but the present moment lasts only a few seconds, and the future is closer than you think.[2] By staying future-focused, you prioritize yourself over fleeting emotions, like feeling you need to give up because you've made a mistake.

When you face setbacks, like a diet not delivering the results you expected, it's easy to feel discouraged. You might have been given unrealistic expectations (like losing ten pounds in five days), and being misled can be tough to process—especially when you've done your best and worked hard for something you really want. While it's important to acknowledge how upsetting this is, you also need to keep the long-term goal in mind. When you focus on the bigger picture, it becomes easier to push past temporary emotions and not confuse them with facts, so you can stay on track.

So if you decide to skip the gym one day because you want to sleep in, that's okay. Life happens, and routines need to be flexible. And if you need to rearrange or miss a workout just once, it's not a big deal. But if it starts happening often, you might need to be stricter about sticking to your schedule. The key is to not let small setbacks throw you off track, and instead, adjust when needed.

Sometimes, you hold onto certain thoughts because they serve a purpose, even if that purpose isn't helpful. For example, maybe a thought like "I'll never be able to do this" feels familiar or comforting in the short term. But when you evaluate, you can find healthier alternatives that move you toward the future you want. By replacing old, limiting thoughts with new, empowering ones, you create a path that leads to progress, success, and clearer thoughts.

CONTINUAL CONTROL

Thoughts come in varying intensities. Sometimes, they're tied to deeper patterns, and other times, "they ain't that deep." If you're struggling with an emotionally charged thought, you can use what you learned from the past few sections in a simple, yet powerful framework called the

ICE Method, designed to help you "cool" those emotionally charged thoughts.

The ICE Method involves three simple steps:

1. Identifying unhealthy thoughts
2. Challenging and changing those thoughts to make them healthier
3. Evaluating how reframing the thoughts will improve your life

Each step aligns with the concepts covered in the last few chapters, and you can use these chapters as guides while you work through reframing emotionally charged thoughts.

While the ICE Method is here to help you identify and correct unhelpful thoughts, it's up to you to keep practicing it. The more you reframe your thoughts, the less mental noise you'll have. And the more you challenge past thoughts, like we did earlier, the easier it will become to reframe them.

So, if you have trouble controlling your emotions and want to cool your responses or stop confusing emotions with facts, keep the momentum going. Practice reflection using the templates at the back of the book to apply the ICE Method to situations where you've previously confused feelings with facts.

By identifying, challenging, and evaluating past thoughts and situations, you'll reduce their intensity and impact so you can learn from them. Eventually, you'll find yourself naturally replacing emotionally driven thoughts with healthier ones in real time.

Here are a few pointers to keep in mind as you continue your journey forward:

- **Awareness Is the First Step.** Recognizing when emotions are influencing your thoughts gives you the power to question them.
- **Mistakes Are Part of the Process.** Improving your mindset is about progress, not perfection. Start small and focus on one area at a time, over time, challenging emotional reasoning will become second nature.
- **Be Kind to Yourself.** Emotions can be triggered by deep-seated beliefs or automatic thoughts, which take time to uncover. Don't stress about recognizing your thoughts immediately. Simply becoming aware of them is a win.

Now, let's look at some "rules" to help you think more clearly and more effectively.

5 RULES OF CLEAR THINK

RULE #1. I HONOR MY WORTH

Self-worth is the foundation of clear, confident thinking. When you believe you're worthy, you set healthy boundaries, take intentional steps toward your goals, and make choices based on your values. When you lack self-worth, you end up stuck, making decisions based on fear, abandoning goals, and not treating yourself with kindness.

Since self-worth is a core belief that often goes unnoticed, you may not realize when you're acting out of alignment. And since you've been taught that buying products, seeking external validation, and following societal norms will make you feel worthy or prove your value, you may not recognize when your actions reflect a deep struggle with self-worth.

The belief that you're not enough leads to behaviors that push you further from what you want and the success you deserve, even when opportunities are within reach. This can show up as:

1. **Procrastination.** Putting off important tasks because deep down you fear you're not worthy or good enough to succeed.

2. **Over-apologizing.** Apologizing excessively for things that don't require an apology because you're unconsciously driven by a need for approval.

3. **People-Pleasing.** Saying "yes" to requests and neglecting your own needs because you think you're being easy going, but really you're trying to avoid rejection or conflict.

4. **Perfectionism.** Setting impossibly high standards because of an internalized belief that you need to be perfect to deserve love and be accepted.

5. **Avoiding Challenges.** Not pursuing opportunities or taking risks because of a deep-set fear that you're not capable or worthy of success.

6. **Self-Criticism.** Constantly focusing on flaws and mistakes, instead of celebrating achievements, because you think you must constantly improve to be worthy of love or success.

7. **Comparison Traps.** Measuring your worth based on external markers like weight, relationship status, or material success, believing that achieving these will validate you.

For example, you might start doubting your partner's loyalty or pushing people away without any seemingly real reason, because deep down you feel you're not worthy of their love or you're afraid that they'll eventually see your "flaws" and leave. You might hesitate to speak up in a meeting or apply for a promotion because you're nervous others will judge you. Or you'll obsess over things like your pants size, marital status, or possessions, even though they don't define your true worth.

To stop the cycle and promote clear thinking, you need to:

- Be value focused
- Set personal boundaries
- Maintain realistic goals

VALUES

Think of values like a centering stone. In life, you're constantly distracted and making countless daily decisions. Values serve as guiding principles to help you stay on track. They ground you, prompting you to pause and reflect so you can focus on what truly matters.

While there's no definitive number of values (some lists include hundreds), you can only realistically focus on three to seven core values at a time. This allows for clarity and balance without becoming overwhelmed.

Too many values dilute focus and make it harder to act consistently, while too few may not fully represent your guiding principles. Read the values listed below and pick at least three that resonate with you:

1. Integrity: honesty, trust, ethical behavior, and order
2. Respect: consideration, fairness, and kindness
3. Responsibility: accountability, dependability, and stewardship
4. Growth: learning, adaptability, innovation, achievement, and intelligence
5. Spirituality: presence, gratitude, and devotion
6. Excellence: quality, mastery, and achievement
7. Connection: relationships, empathy, and community
8. Courage: boldness, perseverance, and resilience
9. Creativity: imagination, originality, expression, and fun
10. Well-being: balance, health, harmony, and mental health
11. Purpose: meaning, contribution, and vision

Take some time to consider what values are most important to you. How can you continue to integrate them into your life? For instance, if you value growth, how will you continue to focus on creating clear thoughts?

_____

_____

_____

_____

_____

PERSONAL BOUNDARIES

Boundaries create a structure that supports your values, priorities, and sense of self. They define how you want to be treated and act as best practices for maintaining overall health and happiness.

Think of personal boundaries like an instruction manual. Just like a manual for a drone will say it can't fly in high winds, yours might say you can't operate on low sleep (which is why you need to be in bed by midnight on work nights).

To set effective boundaries, start by identifying your values and considering what makes you happy and comfortable. For instance, if you're not comfortable sending racy photos to a partner, your boundary would be to not send naked pictures, even if your partner enjoys them. And if you value integrity, your boundary would be to not misrepresent information, even if your boss asks you to.

Boundaries are important because they help you live in alignment and maintain clarity. When you abandon your values, you lose that clarity. If you send intimate pictures because your partner insists, even though it makes you uncomfortable, you're prioritizing their wants over your boundaries.

In doing so, you send yourself the message that other people's preferences matter more than your well-being (that being liked matters more than being true to your-self). Over time, this reduces your self-worth, making you feel like you're not as worthy or deserving as others. It can also lead to codependency, where you excessively seek your partner's approval, using their validation as your centering stone rather than your own values and boundaries.

This unhealthy dynamic creates relationship turmoil, where you experience heightened emotions when your partner pulls away, making it harder to think clearly and recover after a disagreement. This is often seen when people react intensely after a breakup. They aren't thinking clearly because their thoughts are consumed by the need for approval, rather than focusing on themselves.

While you might put other people's needs before yours in small ways like giving them the bigger slice of pizza or offering them the warmer side of the bed, those are acts of love, not compromises that undermine your sense of self.

Remember, it's about balance, not perfection. Boundaries don't have to be rigid. Life is unpredictable, so it's important to be flexible and show yourself compassion when things don't go as planned. The key is to stay consistent with your boundaries but also allow room for grace when circumstances change.

What's important to you? What do you need to feel safe and respected? Once you have clarity on that, you can set limits around your time, energy, and interactions with others. For example, if work-life balance is a priority, you might establish boundaries around not answering emails after a certain hour.

REALISTIC GOALS

Unrealistic goals often stem from outside influences, insecurity, or the pressure to compare yourself to others. It's easy to get caught up in the idea that you need to do more, be more, or have more to measure up. This can lead to setting goals based on what you think you should achieve rather than what you truly want or are capable of.

When your goals are driven by external validation (like impressing others or meeting societal standards), it becomes harder to stay motivated. You end up chasing things that don't align with your values or sense of self-worth.

Here are a few examples of unrealistic goals versus self-worth-centered goals:

Unrealistic Goal: Create a perfect seven-step morning routine to be productive and feel "successful" by societal standards.
Self-worth-centered goal: Develop a morning routine that feels authentic and supportive of your well-being, allowing room for flexibility based on your needs and energy levels.

Unrealistic goal: Lose weight quickly to look like an Instagram influencer.

Self-worth-centered goal: Exercise regularly and intuitively eat nutritious foods to feel healthy and strong.

Unrealistic goal: Achieve a "perfect" work-life balance with no room for mistakes.
Self-worth-centered goal: Prioritize work and personal time based on what helps you thrive, while allowing flexibility for life's unpredictability.

Unrealistic goal: Always be in control and have everything figured out.
Self-worth-centered goal: Embrace imperfection and growth, learning from mistakes while accepting yourself as a work in progress.

Unrealistic goal: Follow trends or societal expectations to feel worthy or successful.
Self-worth-centered goal: Pursue passions and goals that resonate with your values, regardless of external trends or pressure.

Unrealistic goals cloud your judgment and prevent you from thinking clearly about what you truly want and need. The pressure to have a "perfect" routine can leave you overwhelmed and stuck in the pursuit of an unattainable ideal. This hampers your ability to think clearly and adapt to what you actually need on any given day because you're more focused on meeting the expectation rather than honoring your own needs.

Chasing an ideal body image based on external standards makes it difficult to think clearly about what truly serves your health. When you're consumed by comparison, it's easy to lose sight of what makes you feel good in your own body, leading to confusion and poor decision-making.

Trying to be perfect in every area of life clouds your ability to think clearly. When you try to stick to a rigid idea of balance, you get overwhelmed by small mistakes or setbacks, making it harder to stay focused on your true needs and priorities.

The desire for complete control can cloud your judgment and prevent you from seeing the bigger picture. It can make you focus so much on avoiding mistakes or having all the answers that it becomes difficult to learn and grow from experiences, limiting your ability to make clear, thoughtful decisions.

The key to setting meaningful goals is to root them in self-respect and authenticity. Start by thinking about what you want, not what others are doing or what others think you should do. Do you really want that ideal body or do you want to feel confident and comfortable in your own? Do you really need that perfect morning routine or do you just want to make sure you start your day on a healthy note?

When you set unrealistic goals, you'll feel guilty or like you aren't measuring up when really you just set yourself up for failure. Setting realistic goals creates a sense of purpose and makes it easier to stay motivated. Remember, it's not about being perfect; it's about making progress and staying aligned with your priorities. So when things don't go as planned, instead of beating yourself up, acknowledge the setback, learn from it, and keep moving forward knowing that you're worthy of success, no matter the pace.

SELF-WORTH IS KEY

The majority of the time, it's not your abilities holding you back, but an ingrained belief of unworthiness. This belief can be so deeply rooted that you may not even realize it's influencing your emotions, clouding your judgment, and leading to self-sabotaging behaviors.

When you honor your self-worth, you stop overanalyzing, second-guessing, and letting fear dictate your actions. Instead, you trust yourself, filter out insecurity, and make decisions aligned with your true desires. This clarity enables you to set boundaries, prioritize your values, and set realistic goals, creating a cycle that supports your well-being.

The beauty of this journey is that it's ongoing. Each time you choose to honor yourself, you create a ripple effect that impacts everything around you. The more you nurture your worth, the more you'll see your confidence grow, your decisions improve, and your relationships thrive. Keep moving forward, knowing that the process of honoring yourself is always worth the effort—and it transforms your world in ways you may not even expect.

RULE #2. I'M EQ FOCUSED

The idea that emotions are a big part of success started gaining attention in the early '90s. Researchers were trying to figure out why some people were more successful at work than others. They thought IQ would be the key, but they found emotions mattered more than they realized.

This discovery laid the foundation for the concept of emotional intelligence (EQ), which was later defined as the ability to understand and manage one's emotions while also navigating and influencing the emotions of others.[1] The benefits of higher emotional intelligence are numerous, including:

- Stronger relationships and collaboration.
- Higher salary and earning potential.[2]
- Managing stress and staying calm under pressure.

- Improving decision-making by reducing emotional bias.
- Communicating more effectively in personal and professional settings.
- Enhancing resilience and adaptability in the face of challenges.

Traditionally reserved for professionals, EQ is equally important in every area of life. It affects your mindset, which shapes how you see and interact with the world every day. If both thought and emotional intelligence were taught in schools, we would have a kinder, more understanding society, and people would no longer feel stuck or controlled by their emotions.

Improving EQ isn't about suppressing emotions but understanding them and using that insight to make thoughtful decisions. It's about managing emotional impulses, avoiding biases, and communicating effectively —skills that enhance relationships, reduce stress, and improve decision-making.

Before I created thought intelligence (the ability to recognize and manage thoughts), I taught emotional intelligence, and it was here I saw a gap in knowledge. Thoughts drive emotions, and without addressing them, it's difficult to build strong emotional intelligence. At the same time, high EQ supports clear thinking. It helps you stay grounded and intentional in emotionally charged situations, enabling logical, focused decisions. It became clear (no pun intended) that improving EQ would enhance thinking clarity, and clearer thinking would help build emotional intelligence.

While there's enough information about emotional intelligence to fill a few books, here I'll give you a general overview of the four key areas of emotional intelligence with some quick tips to help you start building your EQ and support your efforts to think more clearly.

1. SELF-AWARENESS

Emotional awareness is the foundation of emotional intelligence. It involves recognizing and labeling your emotions, understanding why you're feeling them, and recognizing how they influence your decisions. This awareness helps you identify emotional triggers and ensures that your actions align with your values and goals.

For example, if you're feeling insecure about a decision, recognizing those emotions allows you to step back and assess the situation from a balanced perspective. Ask yourself, "Am I unsure because this isn't a good opportunity, or am I just nervous about uncertainty?" From there, dig deeper into the root cause: *Is it a lack of self-worth or just fear of the unknown?*

Many people struggle with identifying their feelings without judgment, and building emotional awareness can be challenging, especially when we live in an environment where emotions have been labeled as weakness. To begin, start by seeing emotions as a resource, not a downfall, and remember that even people with high emotional intelligence can get stuck understanding why they feel a certain way. EQ is a skill that improves with practice, and reflection combined with an open perspective can help identify what triggers your emotions.

You're already making progress by focusing on your thoughts, as you did with the ICE Method. The more you focus on your thoughts, the easier it will become to understand your emotions, fueling better decision-making and revealing patterns that can be reversed.

Activities for Building Emotional Awareness

- Morning Check-in: Before doing anything (checking your phone, getting out of bed, etc.), pause to ask yourself how you feel. If you feel good, work to maintain that mood. If you're feeling off, avoid making big decisions until you're more centered.
- Primary vs. Secondary Emotions: Reflect on whether your emotions are primary or secondary. For example, if you feel anger, ask yourself if it's hiding sadness. Understanding this distinction helps to address the root cause rather than just the reaction.
- Validate Your Emotions: Practice allowing yourself to feel emotions without judgment. Sometimes, instead of trying to cheer yourself up or fix the situation, it's helpful to simply sit with your feelings. Giving yourself permission to feel

without invalidating or suppressing those emotions can promote deeper emotional understanding.

2. SELF-MANAGEMENT

Emotional management is the second key component of emotional intelligence. It's about finding a balance between feeling and acting and involves regulating your emotions so you don't do something you'll regret. When you're able to manage your emotions, you can pause and assess the situation rather than acting impulsively. This allows you to make decisions that align with your values and goals, helping you avoid knee-jerk reactions that might lead to regret later.

The goal is to prevent emotions from controlling you, enabling you to act in ways that are in your best interest and promote healthier relationships and outcomes. So if you're upset with someone, emotional regulation helps you stay calm and respond thoughtfully, rather than letting frustration lead to a harsh or impulsive comment. Similarly, if you're feeling overwhelmed, emotional management allows you to take a step back, breathe, prioritize tasks, and tackle problems one at a time. This approach helps prevent panic, leading to more effective, rational decision-making.

It sounds simple when reading about it, but emotional regulation can be difficult. Emotions are powerful, and we often avoid them because they bring discomfort. Most unhealthy behaviors like addiction, shopping sprees, or overworking stem from a desire to escape uncomfortable emotions. But managing these emotions instead of avoiding them allows you to regain control and make decisions based on logic rather than emotional impulses, and the more you do it, the easier it becomes.

Activities to Build Emotional Management

- Pause and Breathe: When you start to feel overwhelmed, take a moment to breathe deeply. This will help you calm your emotions and think clearly before reacting.
- Reflect on Past Experiences: Think back to a time when your emotions got the best of you and led to regret. Reflecting on past situations where reacting impulsively caused problems can serve as motivation to pause and manage your emotions more effectively now.
- Reframe Stressful Situations: When you're stressed, ask yourself, "What's the worst that could happen?" By putting things into perspective, you can reduce the emotional weight and approach the situation with more clarity.

3. SOCIAL AWARENESS

Social awareness (a.k.a. empathy) is an important part of emotional intelligence. It means understanding and recognizing the emotions of others, which helps you respond thoughtfully and build better relationships.

When you're able to empathize with someone, it shows that you understand their feelings and can communicate in a way that acknowledges their emotions while keeping your own emotions in check. This leads to healthier, clearer interactions with those around you.

Example 1 (Parenting): If you're a parent and your child is acting out, it might be easy to react quickly with frustration or anger. But by practicing empathy, you pause and try to understand what's causing their behavior. Instead of reacting harshly, you ask, "What's going on?" or "Is something bothering you?" This approach helps you get to the root of the issue, fostering communication and understanding. By focusing on empathy, you create a space for a more positive outcome, strengthening the relationship and teaching your child how to process emotions effectively.

Example 2 (Workplace): If you're a manager with an employee who's underperforming, you might feel frustrated and want to react quickly, perhaps by reprimanding them. But by practicing empathy, you pause and think about why they're struggling. Instead of reacting with anger, you ask, "Is something affecting your work?" This helps you understand their situation and work together on a solution. By focusing on empathy, you handle the situation constructively, leading to a more positive outcome for both the employee, the organization, and your team.

Empathy doesn't mean agreeing with someone; it means understanding their feelings, even if you don't agree with their actions or viewpoint. For example, if a friend is upset, you can empathize by saying, "I understand why you're upset," but still disagree with how they handled a situation. True empathy also respects personal boundaries. You can empathize with someone's perspective but still decide not to continue a relationship if their actions were hurtful. This allows for clear, respectful communication while maintaining your own emotional well-being.

Activities for Building Empathy

- Pause and Listen: When you're talking to someone, focus on really listening to their words. Before responding, take a moment to reflect on what they're saying and ask how they're feeling. This helps you connect better and respond in a way that shows empathy.
- Assume Positive Intent: When someone's actions or words frustrate you, remind yourself that they might not have meant to upset you. Assume that their intentions were positive and try to understand the situation from their perspective. This helps you stay calm and make more thoughtful decisions.
- Practice Empathy in Everyday Interactions: Whether you're talking to a friend, family member, or co-worker, make a habit of asking yourself how they might be feeling. This practice will help you develop a stronger sense of empathy and improve your ability to respond to others with understanding.

4. RELATIONSHIP MANAGEMENT

Influence is the ability to inspire, persuade, and positively impact others and is an essential part of EQ. When you use influence effectively, you help create calm, positive interactions that reduce emotional tension in group settings. This promotes clarity and focus during problem-solving or decision-making. For example, by encouraging collaboration, you can ensure that everyone's perspectives are considered without letting emotions cloud the issue at hand.

Strong influence is rooted in trust and authenticity. When people feel heard and valued, they're less likely to act out of frustration or misunderstanding. This helps to reduce reactive emotional responses, which leads to more thoughtful, logical conversations and decisions.

A key part of influence is perspective-taking. By understanding others' motivations and aligning them with shared goals, you can encourage less emotional bias and more rational thinking. Influence can guide others to look beyond their immediate reactions and consider long-term outcomes, fostering a more balanced approach to decision-making.

Leaders with strong influence often set the tone for emotional dynamics within groups. When they model emotional regulation and clear thinking, they inspire others to follow suit. This leads to an environment where everyone is more likely to think clearly and make decisions based on facts and shared objectives.

Activities for Building Relationship Management/Influence

- Foster Open Communication: In conversations, make sure to listen actively and show that you value the other person's perspective. This helps build trust and encourages more open, rational dialogue.
- Encourage Perspective-Taking: In group discussions, ask people to share their views, then encourage them to think about how those views might connect with the group's overall goals. This helps reduce biases and fosters collaborative decision-making.
- Model Emotional Regulation: The next time you're in a stressful situation, focus on managing your own emotions calmly. By staying composed, you influence others around you to follow suit, creating a more productive, focused environment.

EMOTIONS ARE STRENGTH

Most of us have been told that emotions are a sign of weakness. This message often comes from others dismissing, hiding, or downplaying their feelings—or even making fun of us when we show ours. As a result, many people learn to push their emotions aside instead of figuring out how to manage them.

But when you look at the facts, like how emotional control leads to higher wages and better relationships (and all the benefits that come with those things), it would be more accurate to say, "Emotions are only a weakness for those who don't know how to control them." And as we've seen in the first part of the book, there are a lot of industries that benefit when you don't know how to control your emotions.

By understanding your emotions, you can make logical decisions based on what truly matters, instead of being swept up in temporary feelings. Whether it's resolving conflicts, managing stress, or staying on track toward a goal, EQ helps you handle situations with balance and clarity.

It's not always easy to manage emotions, especially in a world that often discourages emotional awareness. Emotional intelligence is all about growth, and each part of it builds on the others. If you're strong in one area, you can use that strength to improve in others. Over time, this makes it easier to handle challenges and approach life with confidence and balance. The good news is that you're already building EQ by working on your thought habits and separating feelings from facts. The more you practice these skills, the easier it gets to manage your emotions.

RULE #3. I BUILD MY INTUITION

"Trust your gut." "Do what feels right." You're told to follow your instincts and trust your intuition, but you aren't encouraged to be in tune with your emotions. As a result, you can easily confuse anxiety and fear-based emotions with your gut. This leads to impulsive decisions, explosive reactions, or missed opportunities because you mistake emotional noise for truth.

To think clearly, you need to build your intuition and make sure your anxiety is in check. To do this, you need to clearly understand the difference between the two.

WHAT IS INTUITION?

Intuition is often described as a "gut feeling" or the ability to understand something instinctively, without needing detailed analysis. While you're taught to believe intuition is something you're born with and just need to "tap into," the truth is that intuition is shaped by experience. It's a mix of knowledge and past experiences stored in your mind that surfaces when you're in a similar situation, often without you realizing it.

When experts seem to make quick, instinctive judgments, what looks like a gut feeling is actually their brain processing years of knowledge and recognizing patterns they've seen before.[1] These decisions aren't random—they're informed by a lifetime of learning. This is why intuition improves with experience: it's not just instinct, but your brain connecting the dots from what it already knows.

Intuition can be a powerful inner guide. It's that quiet, steady voice that helps you make decisions before your rational mind catches up. When you're aligned with your intuition, you:

- make confident, informed decisions
- stay aligned with your goals and values
- trust yourself even in uncertain situations

Unfortunately, your intuition can get muddled when you confuse it with fear, worry, or stress. These emotions create urgency and alarm, making you mistake anxiety for intuitive insight. This confusion is reinforced by how you were raised—taught to ignore your emotions and never given the chance to learn the difference between anxiety and intuitive feeling.

When you're overwhelmed by emotions, it's easy to think you're following your gut when you're really just reacting to fear. Intuition feels calm and clear. Anxiety, on the other hand, feels restless and uncertain. Here are some other key differences:

INTUITION	ANXIETY
Calm, peace, and natural ease in the body.	Tension, fast heartbeat, and discomfort, often with a sense of unease.
Quiet, confident voice that feels like the truth needing to analyze.	Loud, frantic thoughts filled with worry, doubt, and urgency.
Clear and direct knowing, guiding your actions with certainty.	Confusing and uncertain thoughts that lead to overthinking and hesitation.
Quick, subtle, and only lasts for a short time.	Constant, repetitive thoughts about the future or "what-if" scenarios.
Feels peaceful, true to your values, and right for the situation.	Tense, fearful, and reactive, based on imagined negative outcomes.
Guided by the present moment, fits the situation.	Fueled by past experiences or worry.
Feels confident and peaceful after making a decision.	Doubt and discomfort after a decision, feeling unsettled or regretful.

BUILDING INTUITION

While there are tips to help you tell the difference between intuition and anxiety, the best teacher is experience. You build intuition by putting yourself out there, trying new things, and listening to your body. Your body is always giving you signals, and the more you tune in, the easier it gets to understand what they mean. Here is an example from my life:

Finding the right people to work with can be tough in any field, and book writing is no exception. When I had to choose an important vendor, I wasn't sure about my decision. I felt this knot in my stomach, but I couldn't tell if it was my gut warning me or just anxiety because the decision felt so big. I ended up hiring the vendor, and things didn't work out.

Luckily, you realized early on that you weren't a good match, so not much time was wasted. Looking back, you now know that feeling in your stomach was your intuition trying to tell you something was off.

Yes, mistakes can cost time and money, but you're not just paying for the mistake, you're paying for the lesson. And the more you learn, the less those lessons will cost.

You can make the process faster and smoother (and make less mistakes) by focusing on the activities and perspectives in this book. Here are some other supportive tips:

- Pause and Breathe: Take a moment to ground yourself. Slow, deep breaths can help distinguish between the nervousness of anxiety and the calm clarity of intuition.
- Check Your Body: Intuition tends to feel more relaxed and centered in your body, while anxiety

manifests as tightness or a "flight or fight" response.

- Ask Yourself, "Does this Feel Right?": If the feeling brings calmness, confidence, and a sense of alignment with your values, it's likely intuition. If it brings stress, worry, or fear, it's probably anxiety.
- Write It Down: Journaling your thoughts and feelings can help you analyze them later. Often, when you're in a calm state, you can better assess if the initial feeling was truly intuitive or anxiety-driven.

TRAUMA INFORMED

Building intuition involves validating your emotions and recognizing that there's often a reason for how you feel, even if it's not entirely accurate. This can be difficult if you've experienced trauma, as it can disrupt your ability to trust your gut. Trauma keeps your nervous system on high alert, making it harder to filter out the noise and rely on your instincts, which is why many people who've been through it struggle with anxiety and depression.

You might think people are against you, interpret things negatively, or feel constantly nervous. Even if you logically know there is no reason not to trust someone, those feelings can come from the fact that people you previously trusted didn't treat you with kindness. Walking through that pain is the only way to release it. It hurts in the moment, and there may always be a lingering ache, but facing it head-on is the only way to truly live and move forward.

When I was healing from trauma, trusting my instincts was one of the hardest things for me. My intuition kept telling me to run, and I felt safest when I was completely alone—on my couch, eating takeout, and watching *Gilmore Girls*. Trusting people felt wrong on every level because my intuition had been trained to keep me isolated. At one point, I had to start going against my gut and ignoring that overwhelming urge to run—even when every fiber of my being told me to leave. I used to believe that if something was this hard, it meant it wasn't meant to be. But then I realized the difficulty came from not managing my emotions well.

THE POWER OF INTUITION

When you have a strong sense of intuition, you're able to move through life with more confidence, clarity, and purpose. You're not swayed by doubt or external noise because you trust yourself to make the best decisions you can and to course correct if things don't go as planned.

There's no shortcut to finding your intuition because reconnecting with it means reconnecting with yourself. That journey can be uncomfortable, sad, stressful, or even lonely at times, but it's also one of the most rewarding things you'll ever do. I hope my experiences and words bring you comfort in difficult moments, helping you push through to the great ones.

RULE #4. I CHOOSE THOUGHTFUL RESPONSES

Thoughtful responses help you act with intention and clarity rather than reacting on impulse. They keep you aligned with your goals, improve your emotional intelligence, and strengthen your intuition.

Unfortunately, most of us (myself included) weren't taught the difference between responding with awareness and reacting emotionally. As a result, we often act on impulse, unaware that there's a better approach.

This might look like making snap decisions instead of considering your options or letting small inconveniences throw you off track when what you really need is a moment to pause and reflect on how your actions will impact you long-term.

To think clearly, you need to shift from reacting to responding. That means taking a moment to assess your emotions, calm your mind, and choose a thoughtful course of action—allowing you to move through life with intention, confidence, and control.

WHAT IS A THOUGHTFUL RESPONSE?

Thoughtful responses help us engage with the world in a measured, constructive way that aligns with our deeper intentions. They keep us connected to our values and focused on our goals, leading to more fulfilling and successful interactions.

EMOTIONAL REACTION	THOUGHTFUL RESPONSE
Immediate, instinctive	Deliberate, reflective
Driven by frustration, anger, fear	Guided by awareness and clarity
Impulsive, reactive	Slow, measured
Can escalate conflict	Aims to resolve and understand
Defensive or confrontational	Calm, empathetic
Focused on quick relief	Focused on long-term goals
May lead to regret or tension	Leads to understanding
Ignores broader consequences	Considers long-term impact
Destructive	Constructive

In a heated conversation, instead of reacting with frustration, you pause, take a deep breath, and assess the situation. Then, you respond calmly by saying, "I understand your concern. Let's discuss how we can address this together.'"

When faced with a challenging decision, rather than panicking or making a rushed decision, you pause and think, *It looks like there are several factors to consider here. I'll take some time to weigh the pros and cons.* And if you're forced to make a decision in a rush, while you may feel flustered, you would also have a sense of calm knowing that you're thinking as clearly as you can given the situation and will make the best decision you can with the information you have at the moment.

MAKING THE SWITCH

To shift from reacting to responding, you first need to understand the difference, as you just did above. From there, you can reflect on past situations where you reacted out of emotion and consider how they might have turned out if you'd responded thoughtfully instead.

Let's streamline the process by using the ICE Method we discussed earlier. Before we begin, remember that this isn't about beating yourself up for mistakes but learning from them. Be honest, even if you're not proud of how you acted.

Identify

When you were reading the introduction to this section, did a time where you reacted instead of responded come to mind? What was the situation and what was your reaction? How was that misaligned with your values and goals? How did it end up? Write down or think about it in as much detail as you can.

_____

_____

_____

_____

Challenge

Knowing what you know now about responding instead of reacting and taking a breath before responding, what would you have done differently? How would you have ideally responded and how would that align with your values and goals?

_____

_____

_____

_____

Evaluate

How would your ideal response benefit you in the future and keep you more aligned with your goals?

_____

_____

_____

APOLOGIES EASE

Forgiveness is one of those topics that's often misunderstood. People tend to think it means excusing someone's actions or pretending the hurt didn't happen, but true forgiveness isn't about reconciling or condoning; it's about healing and finding peace—whether or not the other person acknowledges their role in the hurt.

While forgiveness is typically seen as something that benefits the person doing the forgiving, it also helps the person asking for forgiveness. It reduces the emotional intensity of past situations, making it easier to respond more thoughtfully in the future.

Imagine you act impulsively during an emotionally charged moment and accuse someone of something they didn't do. The guilt of hurting them adds to the weight of your frustration, making it harder to move forward. But when you apologize, you face the original emotion head-on and work to ease the guilt with an honest apology. This process reduces the emotional charge, making it easier to process your feelings and avoid reacting the same way next time.

That said, forgiveness doesn't always mean rushing to apologize. Sometimes people need space to process, and respecting their boundaries is just as important as making amends. In the interim, you can focus on understanding what led to the mistake and how to avoid it in the future, since a meaningful apology involves changed behavior.[1]

If your apology isn't accepted, it doesn't mean you're doomed to repeat the same mistake. Forgiving yourself is just as important. We're often harder on ourselves than anyone else, which can create even more emotional pressure. This can lead to overthinking, bigger mistakes, or shutting down entirely. But self-forgiveness reminds us that mistakes are part of learning and growing.

It's important to remember that everyone is working through their own challenges, even if it doesn't seem like it. When someone asks for forgiveness, even if you're not ready to forgive or reconcile, you can respond without reacting. Acknowledge their effort by saying something like, "I appreciate that you're trying, but I'm not ready to forgive right now," or "I can't have a relationship with you at this time, but I see you're trying to grow."

By showing someone else the understanding and support they need, you reinforce that mistakes are opportunities to learn. And when you extend kindness to others, even when it's difficult, you're ultimately giving that same kindness to yourself. This act of compassion, though challenging, is one of the greatest gifts you can offer—to yourself and to others.

QUICK TIPS FOR PRACTICING NON-REACTIVE RESPONSES

- **Pause Before Responding.** Take a deep breath, count to ten, or step away briefly to process your emotions.

- **Use Grounding Techniques.** Try box breathing, repeating "I am safe" to yourself, or taking a short walk to create space between your reaction and response.
- **Align with Your Values.** Before reacting, ask yourself if your response reflects your core values and the person you want to be.
- **Use "I" Statements.** Express feelings without blame by saying, "I feel frustrated when…" instead of, "You always…"
- **Stay Calm Under Pressure.** Lower your voice, slow your speech, and focus on problem-solving rather than reacting emotionally.

RESPONDING IN ALIGNMENT

Clear thinking helps you recognize the link between your thoughts and emotions while breaking the cycle of automatic reactions. By becoming more aware of your thought patterns, you can choose intentional responses instead of impulsive reactions.

Shifting from reacting to responding brings you clarity, calmness, and confidence, ensuring your actions align with your values and goals. Thoughtful responses help you manage emotional triggers rather than being controlled by them, leading to better communication, healthier relationships, and more intentional decisions.

Making the switch from reacting to responding can be tough, especially since it has probably been a habit your whole life. I wish there was a quick fix or shortcut to stop the impulse right away, but that's just not how it works. It takes some trial and error. But just like any growth process, you'll learn a lot about yourself and gain clarity along the way.

RULE #5. I LEARN FROM MY MISTAKES

Efficiency tips are a dime a dozen. You're taught to use resources like planners and scheduling techniques to make the most of your time, budgeting skills to manage your money effectively, and entire industries are built around teaching how to optimize business operations.

But you're rarely (if ever) taught to use your internal resources like your emotions or intuition effectively, and you're steered away from using some of the most valuable resources you have: your mistakes.

Mistakes are commonly considered failures and something you need to be ashamed of, hide, or run away from. But mistakes are actually a great resource. They're a treasure trove of key insights and bring immense value if you recognize their potential. Not learning from mistakes or being ashamed of them would be like being ashamed of winning the lottery or finding a chest of gold coins.

Sure, drunk texting your ex or waving at someone who wasn't actually waving at you is more embarrassing than winning the lottery, but when you play it right, there's a lot you can learn—like putting your phone down after a few drinks or owning simple mistakes, knowing that everyone has their awkward moments.

This ties back to your self-worth. When you view the natural process of growth (learning through trial and error) as something to be ashamed of, you end up feeling ashamed for simply existing. You cut yourself off from life's true meaning and from reaching your potential.

There isn't much to strive for at that point. And without a sense of purpose, you get lost in unhelpful coping mechanisms, meaningless arguments with strangers online, obsessing over celebrities' dating lives and breakups, binge drinking, and shopping.

REVERSE ENGINEERING

To learn from your mistakes, you can embrace a few mindset shifts, like viewing them as opportunities for growth rather than reasons to hide under the covers and never come out again.

By openly communicating your embarrassment and finding humor in simple mistakes, you normalize small errors and move forward. So if you accidentally blurt out "love you" to your boss at the end of a work call, instead of entertaining the impulse to quit your job, you would accept that silly things happen. You might say, "Whoops, my bad! I do think you're great, though!" and laugh it off.

But then there are mistakes that you can't laugh off or seem to shake, no matter how you look at them. The ones that keep you up at night and pop into your mind at the most inopportune moments. For these, you need more than just a shift in perspective—you need to reverse engineer.

Reverse engineering is a method of breaking down a mistake to understand and learn from it. In this case, instead of challenging a mistake with a new perspective (like in the ICE Method), you'll focus on how you wish things had turned out. Then, you'll work backward to identify the lessons and actions needed to grow from it.

Think of a mistake that you really regret. Maybe you pulled money out of the stock market because you panicked, only to see the stock skyrocket afterward. Or perhaps you cheated on someone you loved because you felt vulnerable, and now you deeply regret your actions.

Now, think of how you wish the situation turned out. Ask yourself: How would you have *ideally* handled the situation? In the case of the stock market, the ideal would have been managing your anxiety and leaving your portfolio untouched. In the case of infidelity, the ideal would have been addressing your insecurities in healthier ways and remaining faithful.

From there you can determine actionable steps toward the ideal. What actions can I take now to correct your mistake or work toward a better outcome? For the stock market mistake: The opportunity for those gains is gone, so you can't change the past. However, you can commit to learning from the experience like refraining from hasty investment decisions in the future or educating yourself about emotional triggers in investing.

And while you can't undo the infidelity, you can apologize sincerely to your partner and ask what they need to move forward, if they think reconciliation is possible. Simultaneously, you can work on your growth, like seeking therapy or practicing self-reflection to address the vulnerabilities that led to your actions and prevent self-sabotaging behaviors in the future.

Lastly, you can focus on mental actions for healing. This includes working to accept the situation, acknowledging that the mistake happened and that no matter how badly you want to, you can't change the past.

It's also a great opportunity to practice sitting with your thoughts and allowing them to pass without attaching too much energy to them. For example, if you find yourself spiraling into catastrophic thinking (*I'll never get over this*), you would remind yourself that you've worked through tough situations before. And you would acknowledge that negative-leaning thoughts don't help and only hold you back.

Here is the process summarized in simple steps:

1. **Identify the mistake** that's causing you regret.

2. **Visualize the ideal outcome**—how you wish things had turned out.
3. **Determine actionable steps** to move closer to that ideal, even if it's just committing to learning and growth for the future.
4. **Accept the mistake** as part of being human and work on emotional resilience through mindfulness, self-compassion, and letting go of unhelpful thoughts.

By breaking down your mistakes and focusing on what you can learn from them, you transform regret into a powerful tool for growth and self-improvement.

HAPPY LITTLE ACCIDENTS

It's hard being human. It doesn't need to be, but current culture makes sure it is. You're not taught how to use your greatest resources (your thoughts, emotions, and mistakes), and, in turn, they can feel like they're working against you. You're taught to be critical of yourself, to hate your flaws, and in that misguidance, you end up beating yourself up for your mistakes. Ironically, that's an even bigger mistake because self-compassion is the foundation of learning and growth.[1]

Remember that it's okay to feel disappointed in yourself for something you've done without letting it define your worth. You can be sorry for a mistake without letting it consume your life. And yes, you're allowed to be happy, even if you've done something you regret.

The frustrating reality is that sometimes you need to make the same mistake several times before the lesson really sticks. But the good news is that each time you repeat a mistake, you tend to repeat it with a little less severity, and each time, you learn a little more. Over time, you'll reduce those behaviors, and eventually, new mistakes will take their place. The difference is that these new mistakes will feel less emotionally draining. You'll reach a point where, while you still make mistakes, they'll be minimal and nothing worth losing sleep over.

CONCLUSION: STEPPING INTO YOUR POWER

The look of confusion on people's faces when they hear I don't like the gym always cracks me up.

> But you go all the time.
>
> Yeah, so?
>
> That means you love it.
>
> No.

The truth is, I don't like the gym, but I love the benefits I get from it. And since I'm being honest here, I don't really enjoy the writing process either. I try to make it as enjoyable as possible, but it's holding the final book in my hands and reading reviews about how something I wrote helped someone that keeps me going. Sometimes, I lose sight of that and end up wasting time scrolling on social media when I should be working. But then I get back on track by reminding myself of the end goal.

Same goes for walking. Sometimes I love it—the different sights, the funny moments like seeing people yelling or fighting in the street (I live in Philly, after all). Other times, I'd rather watch paint dry. But I make myself go for walks, especially when I don't feel mentally well, because I know it will help me feel better in the long run.[1]

Sometimes we just need to remind ourselves that doing our best now will put us further ahead than if we get caught up in emotions and don't try. Other times, we need to think toward the future and realize that while sleeping in feels good, working out and accomplishing a goal will feel even better.

The consequences of confusing feelings for facts aren't just about not accomplishing goals—they're about losing ourselves, missing out on connections, hurting the people we love, and pushing away those who could help us grow.

Learning how to control your thoughts and emotions is power, and you're already stepping into it. Look at how far you've come. You've learned to pause and assess your thoughts, question whether your emotions are leading you astray, and choose a clearer, more logical path. You've practiced identifying when emotional reasoning takes hold and learned to challenge those automatic responses.

Not only personal power but also the power of human connection is the most powerful force in the world. This entire world is built on it. Our connections become deeper, more impactful, and more genuine when we're closer to ourselves, focusing on our thoughts and emotions, and making sure they aren't distorting our perception of the world.

Oftentimes, people try to connect by arguing. They don't know any other way to do it, or they're too nervous to be vulnerable—understandable, since emotions are often used against us. Corporations exploit them to control us, and public figures gain popularity by teaching others how to manipulate us.

When we connect over the fact that we live in an environment that often pits us against each other and encourages us to be our own enemies, we can bond over the struggle to stay real in a world that pushes us to focus on trivial things.

We were taught that bravery means buying something or defending a political view online. But true bravery is accepting our thoughts and emotions, owning our mistakes, and learning from them. It's also about extending grace to others when they make mistakes, while understanding that grace and empathy don't require us to keep them in our lives.

Leaning into your thoughts and emotions instead of escaping them is hard. I still struggle with it. It's uncomfortable to talk through things instead of ignoring them and telling yourself to "get over it." Sometimes, it can feel like those emotions will never go away. There have been times in my life when I've asked myself, "If emotions are meant to help me, why are they so painful?"

Then I realized that the emotions weren't the problem; the real issue was my ability to identify and understand what they were telling me. While I'm grateful for how my life turned out, it would have been much easier if I had learned earlier what I've shared with you here. I hope I've helped bring you some ease and clarity, not just in your thoughts, but in your life.

Cheers to you and a path forward that is clearer, stronger, and more intentional. Keep moving ahead with confidence, knowing that mistakes are part of the process. You are doing the best you can, and with time, consistency, and patience, you will make your thoughts and emotions work for you.

I'll leave you with a quote that really resonated with me. In the fifth season of *Buffy the Vampire Slayer*, Buffy is about to sacrifice her life for her sister Dawn. Buffy leaves her with this:

"You have to take care of each other. You have to be strong. Dawn, the hardest thing in this world... is to live in it... Be brave."[2]

Stay golden.

TEMPLATES

ICE METHOD

Situation Nickname: _____

Identify

Describe the situation in much detail as you can. How are you confusing feelings for facts? Can you identify the thoughts behind the feelings?

_____

_____

_____

_____

_____

_____

Challenge

What is the source of the thought? Can you think of alternative perspectives and viewpoints? Is the thought is helpful?

_____

_____

_____

_____

_____

_____

_____

Evaluate

What actions can you take to improve the situation? How will reducing emotional reasoning helps you achieve your goals (and how good that will feel)? Are there obstacles that are preventing change?

_____

_____

_____

_____

_____

_____

NOTES:

ICE METHOD

Situation Nickname: _____

Identify
Describe the situation in much detail as you can. How are
you confusing feelings for facts? Can you identify the
thoughts behind the feelings?

_____

_____

_____

_____

_____

_____

Challenge
What is the source of the thought? Can you think of alternative perspectives and viewpoints? Is the thought is
helpful?

_____

_____

_____

_____

_____

_____

_____

Evaluate

What actions can you take to improve the situation? How will reducing emotional reasoning helps you achieve your goals (and how good that will feel)? Are there obstacles that are preventing change?

_____

_____

_____

_____

_____

_____

NOTES:

ICE METHOD

Situation Nickname: _____

Identify
Describe the situation in much detail as you can. How are you confusing feelings for facts? Can you identify the thoughts behind the feelings?

_____

_____

_____

_____

_____

_____

Challenge
What is the source of the thought? Can you think of alternative perspectives and viewpoints? Is the thought is helpful?

_____

_____

_____

_____

_____

_____

_____

Evaluate

What actions can you take to improve the situation? How
will reducing emotional reasoning helps you achieve
your goals (and how good that will feel)? Are there obstacles that are preventing change?

_____

_____

_____

_____

_____

_____

NOTES:

ICE METHOD

Situation Nickname: _____

Identify

Describe the situation in much detail as you can. How are you confusing feelings for facts? Can you identify the thoughts behind the feelings?

_____

_____

_____

_____

_____

_____

Challenge

What is the source of the thought? Can you think of alternative perspectives and viewpoints? Is the thought is helpful?

_____

_____

_____

_____

_____

_____

_____

Evaluate

What actions can you take to improve the situation? How will reducing emotional reasoning helps you achieve your goals (and how good that will feel)? Are there obstacles that are preventing change?

_____

_____

_____

_____

_____

_____

NOTES:

ICE METHOD

Situation Nickname: _____

Identify

Describe the situation in much detail as you can. How are you confusing feelings for facts? Can you identify the thoughts behind the feelings?

_____

_____

_____

_____

_____

_____

Challenge

What is the source of the thought? Can you think of alternative perspectives and viewpoints? Is the thought is helpful?

_____

_____

_____

_____

_____

_____

_____

Evaluate

What actions can you take to improve the situation? How will reducing emotional reasoning helps you achieve your goals (and how good that will feel)? Are there obstacles that are preventing change?

_____

_____

_____

_____

_____

_____

NOTES:

NOTES

THE POWER OF CLEAR THINKING

1. Noonan (1990), p. 3. The most vivid and memorable description I found for this concept: "Without exaggeration, the human body can be seen as an elaborate machine occupied and operated by the nervous system for the primary purpose of keeping the nervous system alive and moving about. Without it, the body is nothing more than a skin bag filled with bones and exotic meats."
2. Dajose, L. (2024, December 17). Thinking slowly: The paradoxical slowness of human behavior. *Caltech.* https://www.caltech.edu/about/news/thinking-slowly-the-paradoxical-slowness-of-human-behavior
3. West, M. (2022, July 29). Maslow's hierarchy of needs: Uses and criticisms. *Medical News Today.* https://www.medicalnewstoday.com/articles/maslows-hierarchy-of-needs
4. Someone responding strongly or with hostility because they aren't thinking clearly can explain their reaction, but it doesn't excuse it. They are still responsible for their actions.
5. Hu, C. (2024, February 21). Why writing by hand is better for memory and learning. *Scientific America.* https://www.scientificamerican.com/article/why-writing-by-hand-is-better-for-memory-and-learning/

IMPORTANCE OF THOUGHTS AND EMOTIONS

1. Beyoncé. (2011). Run the world (girls) [Track 12 on 4]. Columbia Records.
2. Gangemi, A., Dahò, M., & Mancini, F. (2021). Emotional reasoning and psychopathology. *Brain Sciences, 11*(4), 471. https://doi.org/10.3390/brainsci11040471
3. While the past can teach valuable lessons, it can also mislead us when we mistake past patterns for present realities. These

patterns are often shaped by past experiences, including our environment, upbringing, or trauma.

IDENTIFYING CLOUDINESS

1. Greene, R. (1998).
2. Next time you're watching TV, try to identify the target audience. You can often do this by observing the commercials and considering who would typically buy the products. For example, soap operas were specifically targeted toward stay-at-home mothers and housewives, who were often the primary consumers for household products. The term "soap opera" originated from the fact that many of these daytime dramas were originally sponsored by soap manufacturers, like Procter & Gamble, who used the shows to advertise their products.
3. Straits Research. (2024, September 27). *Neuromarketing market size, share & trends analysis report by technology, end-use industry, and region: Forecasts, 2024-2032*. Straits Research. https://straitsresearch.com/report/neuromarketing-market
4. Mad Men. (2007). The wheel (Season 1, Episode 13) [TV series episode]. In M. Weiner (Executive producer), *Mad Men*. AMC. Watch *Mad Men* and pay attention to how advertising plays with emotions. In the episode "The Wheel," Don Draper explains how advertising uses feelings like love to influence us. This is just one example from the show, but Draper brings up this idea a lot, showing how marketers can shape how you think about words and emotions. Watching this episode will give you a better idea of how companies use emotional triggers to impact our decisions. Understanding this can help us take control of our choices and focus on what really matters.

SEEING THROUGH THE FOG

1. Perley. (2017, April 22). *The dangers of sensationalist media*. The Organization for World Peace. https://theowp.org/reports/the-dangers-of-sensationalist-media/
2. The "Whoosh Effect" is when you don't see progress from diet and workouts for a while, then suddenly notice a big change. It's thought to happen when your body holds onto water while losing fat, and then releases it all at once. Other factors like metabolism,

sleep, stress, and consistency also play a role in how fast you see results.

3. FBI National Press Office. (2024, June 10). *FBI releases 2024 quarterly crime report and use-of-force data update*. FBI. https://www.fbi.gov/news/press-releases/fbi-releases-2024-quarterly-crime-report-and-use-of-force-data-update

4. Daily News. (2020, June 7). *No one is safe* [Cover headline, Facebook post]. Facebook. https://www.facebook.com/story.php?story_fbid=10157354933432541&id=268914272540&p=30&_rdr

EVALUATING THE BENEFITS

1. Perley. (2017, April 22). *The dangers of sensationalist media.* The Organization for World Peace. https://theowp.org/reports/the-dangers-of-sensationalist-media/

2. Tolle. (1997), p. 48.

RULE #2. I'M EQ FOCUSED

1. Urquijo, I., Extremera, N., & Azanza, G. (2019). The contribution of emotional intelligence to career success: Beyond personality traits. *International Journal of Environmental Research and Public Health, 16*(23), 4809. https://doi.org/10.3390/ijerph16234809

2. Sanchez-Gomez, M., Breso, E., & Giorgi, G. (2021). Could emotional intelligence ability predict salary? A cross-sectional study in a multioccupational sample. *International Journal of Environmental Research and Public Health, 18*(3), 1322. https://doi.org/10.3390/ijerph18031322

RULE #3. I BUILD MY INTUITION

1. Gladwell (2005), p.7-12. Gladwell introduces the concept of "thin-slicing," where people make quick, accurate judgments based on limited information and demonstrates how experts rely on their subconscious processing of patterns and experience to make quick judgments without deliberate analysis.

RULE #4. I CHOOSE THOUGHTFUL RESPONSES

1. Buffy the Vampire Slayer. (1998). The wish (Season 3, Episode 9) [TV series episode]. In J. Whedon (Executive producer), Buffy the Vampire Slayer. 20th Century Fox. This episode is great at highlighting the complexities of seeking forgiveness and the importance of respecting personal boundaries during emotional healing. Oz expresses to Willow that her repeated apologies are more about alleviating her own guilt than addressing his feelings. He tells her that he's already heard her apologies and needs time alone to process their relationship, emphasizing that it's not his responsibility to make her feel better.

RULE #5. I LEARN FROM MY MISTAKES

1. When I was managing a team, I would always tell them: The biggest mistake you can make is not learning from your mistakes, and I live by that motto myself.

CONCLUSION: STEPPING INTO YOUR POWER

1. Wang, T. (2018, October 22). Taking your brain out for a walk. Iroquoia Bruce Trail Club. https://iroquoia.on.ca/index.php/2018/10/22/taking-your-brain-out-for-a-walk/#:~:text=While%20walking%20we're%20always,fit%20hit%20and%20brain%20integration
2. Buffy the Vampire Slayer. (2000). The gift (Season 5, Episode 22) [TV series episode]. In J. Whedon (Executive producer), Buffy the Vampire Slayer. 20th Century Fox.

REFERENCES AND FURTHER READING

REFERENCES

Gladwell, M. (2005). *Blink: The power of thinking without thinking*. Little, Brown and Company.

Greene, R. (1998). *The 48 laws of power*. Viking.

Noonan, D. (1990). *Neuro: Life on the frontlines of brain surgery and neurological medicine*. Ballantine Books.

Tolle, E. (1997). *The power of now: A guide to spiritual enlightenment*. Namaste Publishing.

FURTHER READING

Emotional Intelligence

Bradberry, T., & Greaves, J. (2009). *Emotional intelligence 2.0*. TalentSmart.

Carnegie, D. (1998). *How to win friends and influence people*. Dale Carnegie Books.

Goleman, D. (2005). *Emotional intelligence: Why it can matter more than IQ* (10th anniversary ed.). Bantam Books.

Thoughts and Therapy

Burns, D. D. (2006). *When panic attacks: The new, drug-free anxiety therapy that can change your life*. Harmony.

Greenberger, D., & Padesky, C. A. (2015). *Mind over mood: Change how you feel by changing the way you think* (2nd ed.). Guilford Publications.

McKay, M., Wood, J. C., & Brantley, J. (2019). *The dialectical behavior therapy skills workbook: Practical DBT exercises for learning mindfulness, interpersonal effectiveness, emotion regulation, and distress tolerance*. New Harbinger Publications.

Trauma

Bancroft, L. (2003). *Why does he do that? Inside the minds of angry and controlling men.* Penguin.

Herman, J. L. (2015). *Trauma and recovery: The aftermath of violence – From domestic abuse to political terror.* Hachette UK.

Miller, A. (1997). *The drama of the gifted child: The search for the true self* (R. Ward, Trans.; 3rd ed.). Basic Books.

AUTHOR'S NOTE

Clear Think is the third book in the Thoughtbook series and with each book I grow—not just as a writer but in my mindset too.

Unpacking these thought processes means facing my own flaws, which is not always easy. But I hope my honesty shows that sometimes, confusing feelings for facts and making decisions based on emotion rather than logic is a normal part of being human, even for those who teach these topics.

ACKNOWLEDGEMENTS

Thank you to those who share their mental health struggles and to those who are working to gain control of their thoughts. You keep me going.

To everyone who contributed to this book, including editors, designers, alpha and beta readers.

To my friend Dino for helping me think clear.

And thank you to Oz. Your support means the world to me.

Clear Think

Lyndsey Getty

Thoughts
Are
Better
Shared

A Book Club Guide

a letter to readers

Hey there,

My favorite part of *Clear Think* is the examples of Dorothy, Rose, and Blanche. As someone who's watched their fair share of *The Golden Girls*, I could picture them in their house, caught up in their antics, and Sophia delivering the perfect one-liner. I hope this lighthearted approach made this process a little easier for you.

While I kept it casual here, emotional reasoning can be very powerful and hard to overcome. So be kind to yourself, and know that when you look for clarity, you will find it.

Thank you so much for reading, and I hope you enjoy discussing your favorite parts of the book.

-Lyndsey

discussion guidelines

These guidelines create a foundation for healthy and thoughtful discussions, while ensuring participants feel supported and respected.

1. **Confidentiality is Key.** What's said in the discussion stays in the discussion. This creates a safe space for all participants to share their thoughts and feelings openly without fear of judgment or gossip.
2. **Respect All Perspectives.** Everyone has different experiences and viewpoints. Listen actively and respectfully, even if you don't agree. Avoid interrupting and make space for others to speak.
3. **No Fixing or Advising.** Unless someone asks for advice, avoid jumping in with solutions. The goal is to share and listen, not to solve or "fix" each other's problems.
4. **Mental Health Awareness.** If someone expresses distress or seems in need of help, gently encourage them to reach out to their therapist or call a mental health hotline (such as the **Suicide & Crisis Lifeline: 988**). The book club is a space for discussion, not professional mental health support.
5. **Nonjudgmental Space.** Avoid judgmental language and tone. This includes refraining from criticizing others' thoughts, opinions, or personal experiences.

6. **Participation Is Encouraged, but Optional.**
   While everyone is encouraged to participate, it's
   okay if someone wants to pass on a question or
   doesn't feel ready to share. Participation should
   be voluntary and without pressure.
7. **Keep it Constructive.** Constructive discussions
   help us grow, while negativity can hinder open
   communication. Focus on productive, thoughtful
   sharing and be mindful of how your words
   impact others

Constructive feedback offers thoughtful and respectful
responses creating a supportive environment for discussion. It looks like:

- **Acknowledging contributions:** "I really
  appreciated your interpretation of that chapter.
  It made me think differently about the concept."
- **Offering friendly suggestions:** "Could the
  theme you mentioned be expanded by
  considering other viewpoints?"
- **Encouraging dialogue:** "What you said was
  interesting! I'd love to hear more about how you
  think that connects other areas in the book."

discussion questions

1. What did you know about emotional reasoning and confusing feelings for facts before reading *Clear Think*?

2. How has letting emotions cloud your judgment impacted your life? Are there any examples that came to mind while reading the book?

3. What types of situations or emotions tend to trigger emotional reasoning for you?

4. When reading the stories of Dorothy, Rose, and Blanche, which one resonated with you most? Why?

5. Reflect on the "Identify" section and environmental influences. Were you surprised by how organizations profit from emotional messaging? Where do you notice emotional marketing in your life?

6. Can you think of examples in your life or in society where emotions are dismissed or looked down upon? How do you think this perception affects people's ability to manage their emotions?

7. What do you think will be your biggest challenge in overcoming emotional reasoning?

8. What specific strategies or exercises from the book do you find most helpful? How can you add these into your daily routine?

9. How can practicing emotional intelligence benefit you in both personal and professional settings?

10. How do you think increasing emotional and thought intelligence will improve daily interactions and relationships?
11. Were there any key moments or concepts that resonated with you? If so, what were they?

RESOURCES

The information and advice in this book are not a substitute for therapeutic or medical care. Please seek professional help if you believe you may have a condition. If you or someone you care about needs support or someone to talk to, here are two key resources that can help:

Suicide & Crisis Lifeline
A free, confidential 24/7 hotline for anyone in crisis or emotional distress.
988
988lifeline.org

The National Domestic Violence Hotline
A free, confidential 24/7 hotline for anyone experiencing domestic violence or questioning their relationship.
1-800-799-SAFE (7233)
thehotline.org

ABOUT THE AUTHOR

PHOTO BY: Zave Smith

Lyndsey Getty is the creator of Thought Intelligence and founder of The Thought Method Company. She lives in Philadelphia, Pennsylvania.

thoughtmethod.com
@thoughtmethod:

Write to Us!
I'd love to hear about your experience with *Clear Think* and how it has helped you (or how you think we can improve). Email me at lyndsey@thoughtmethod.com.

Your Voice Matters!
Please help others discover *Clear Think* by leaving a review on Amazon. Reviews not only helps new readers but also supports indie authors like me.

For more books and updates:
thoughtmethod.com

The Thoughtbook Series

Overthink

calm thoughts

Stop overthinking and boost confidence.
Build helpful thought patterns.
Control your thoughts.

lyndsey getty

Middle Think

balanced thoughts

Stop all or nothing thinking.
Build a balanced mindset.
Overcome perfectionism.

lyndsey getty

Clear Think

clear thoughts

Stop emotions from clouding your judgement.
Stay levelheaded under pressure.
Make smarter decisions.

lyndsey getty

Big Think

empowered thoughts

Remove mental blockers.
Grow and unlock your potential.
Build confidence and step into your power.

lyndsey getty

Overthink: Calm Thoughts

OVERWHELMED BY CONSTANT MENTAL CHATTER? TRIED EVERYTHING TO QUIET YOUR MIND BUT NOTHING WORKS?

Overthink offers innovative strategies to help you silence mental noise and regain control of your thoughts. Instead of shutting them down, you'll learn to think in a way that truly serves you. Drawing on a decade of research and insights from hundreds of overthinkers, this practical guide explains why common advice often falls short and provides a smarter approach to calm, effective thinking.

With relatable examples and hands-on techniques, *Overthink* delivers valuable insights on every page, including:

- How your thoughts and unconscious mind work
- The unproductive thoughts that keep you stuck
- A simple three-step method to reclaim your mind
- Ways to build confidence and a growth mindset
- Practical strategies to increase your success

This isn't just about silencing your thoughts. It's about transforming them into a powerful tool for clarity, confidence, and purposeful action. *Overthink* isn't just a book; it's a roadmap to a calmer, sharper, and more empowered mind.

Middle Think: Balanced Thoughts

DOES YOUR MIND JUMP BETWEEN EXTREMES, PERFECTIONISM, ALL-OR-NOTHING THINKING, FEELING LIKE THINGS WON'T GET BETTER?

Middle Think offers a powerful yet simple approach to breaking free from these mental traps. Instead of getting stuck in rigid thought patterns, you will learn how to embrace a balanced mindset that fosters clarity, confidence, and resilience.

With relatable examples and actionable strategies, this practical guide helps you shift from extreme thinking to a more flexible, realistic perspective. Key takeaways, include:

- How extreme thinking affects emotions, decisions, and relationships
- Practical techniques to recognize and reframe unhelpful thoughts
- Simple exercises to build mental balance and reduce stress
- Strategies to strengthen resilience and improve self-awareness
- Tools to navigate life's complexities with a clearer, steadier mindset

This is not about suppressing your thoughts, it is about transforming them. *Middle Think* gives you the tools to move beyond extremes and build a mindset that works for you, not against you.

Big Think: Empowered Thoughts

ARE YOUR BELIEFS LIMITING YOUR POTENTIAL? DO MENTAL BLOCKERS AND THOUGHT HABITS HOLD YOU BACK?

Big Think reveals how deeply ingrained beliefs shape your choices, limit your growth, and keep you stuck in old patterns.

Through real-world examples and a simple three-step process, this book helps you identify, challenge, and replace mental blockers with empowering new perspectives.

Packed with practical advice, you'll uncover the beliefs holding you back, build confidence in your decisions, and create new opportunities for growth. You'll also learn how to:

• Find your voice and advocate for yourself
• Break free from external expectations
• Embrace who you are and seek internal validation
• Turn struggles into growth opportunities
• Release shame and build connections

With actionable strategies and relatable insights, *Big Think* helps you move past limitations and step into your full potential. It's time to rewire your mindset and take control of your future.